Salty

D1400334

Aleta L Williams

www.alanasbookline.org

I'm Aleta aka West Coast DivaHotPen. I self published my titles through my company "Alana's Book Line!" Writing for me is more of a hobby; a stepping stone to get to where God is trying to take me. My calling is to give inspiration to young ladies and women who can relate to where I come from. I went from being a motherless child... to an angry teen... a gangster chick....and now I'm a diva out to please the Lord and uplift others. I write true2life street tales with an inspirational bang. I feel in order to be a voice, a voice that's heard, and understood I have to give the real and its gets no realer then the tales I write. I thank you for taking the time to get to know me.

Enjoy!

Warning this book is filled with str8 drama...........

Salty © Copyright 2012 Aleta L Williams

Printed in the United States of America

ISBN 978-1475061413

LCCN: On File

Cover Design/Graphic: SoSo Boston
http://www.facebook.com/sosographics

Cover Model: Bryanna Alize (Brie Beautie)
http://www.facebook.com/brie.b.beautie

Editor: LaMia Ashley

mommamia_08232@yahoo.com

For wholesale orders, contact the author: Aleta L Williams via email lana_books@yahoo.com Mail Orders in the amount of $15.00 USD to Post Office Box 59087 Los Angeles, CA 90059

This book is dedicated to my three babies: Porshay, Anthony, and Miracle. It is because of you mommy stay on her grind. My mother Virginia Ann Thomas and Godmother Cherry, I love and miss you... Thanks for watching over me. To my dad, thanks for always being there. And to my readers....I appreciate you all so much; that's why I dedicated this book to you ☺

Acknowledgments

First I'd like to give thanks to God who is the head of my life. To my pastor for helping me see that God is the reason and that he always has and always will be there for me. To my husband Taboo, I thank you for your continued support. I am so glad that "we" found a way to make it do what it do...the two of us "Chump Change Production and Alana's Book Line" is going places...#Yup... straight to the top!!!! I thank you for my babies; without those three I may not be as determined. A special shot out to my Dub and Hub (Watts and Compton) Divas and Gents: Bridget Davis, Nikki Jay, Dorothy Jenkins, Sherika Nicole, Aja Unconditional Love, Shakeia Law, Kenyanda Reddy, Alysas aka OSO, M&M, Gary, Yo Landa, Khalilah Barber, my HG for life Faniki, my little big HG Pooh, and, sooo many more..... I love and appreciate you all! To all my family and friends thanks for being you.

Shout out to those in the Industry that don't mind supporting and helping a New Author Like Me.........**Karen Williams, Urban Books author (you have too many to name☺), Cash, author of Trust No Man 1, 2&3 and Bonded by Blood, Kre, author of The Game Don't Love Nobody, Sha Dow, author of Fyast Life, Gloria Lathen, author of E.M.O.T.I.O.N.S and Your Purpose Is Greater Than Your Pain, Katrina, author of The Balcony View, Nita Bee over at Steamy Trails, Renda Rose, author of God's Grace and Mercy, Emmanuel Brown, author of I am Royalty and CEO of Seeinggrowth, Mz. Robinson, author of the Love, Lust, & Lies series. #YouGuysRock!!!**

Prologue- A Few Months Back

Locke High School, Watts, CA

Jazz sat in her 7th period, Advance class, aggravated by the jealous females who thought it was cool to get on her bad side. Despite the smirks and subliminal messages, she continued to keep her focus on the teacher. No matter what she did out of school, hanging out with her older cousin, sometimes drinking and smoking, she refused to allow anything or anyone to stop her from getting an education.

"Can anyone tell me four types of defense mechanisms?" The petite teacher asked.

None of the students raised their hands. They went on talking about everything but what was important, which was learning all they could so they would have a shot at graduating, and a choice to get out the ghetto. The teacher looked at Jazz. She knew she could get the correct answers from her but the expression on Jazz's face read, "why me?" And besides, why did Jazz always have to answer? Didn't the other kids learn anything?

"I know," one boy yelled out.

"What is it, Deonta?" asked the teacher.

"Slap the shit of that bitch!"

Almost the entire class burst into laughter. The teacher went from a pale white to a blush red.

"Deonta, go to the office now." She demanded, pointing at the door.

The boy got up and walked out. Once the class settled down, the teacher repeated her question. This time she spoke with authority.

"I need four of you to give me four types of defense mechanisms. If I don't get any volunteers then I will call on you. If the four that I call on do not answer correctly, then you all will have an essay to do; thirty pages." She paused and looked at the students with pity. She couldn't understand why the kids didn't take their education seriously. She wanted to blame the parents for not instilling the importance of an education, but these students needed to take responsibility for their own actions. After all they were high school students. "Now do I have any volunteers?"

Jazz didn't have time for extra work. Her weekends were for her to chill and have fun. In her opinion, 95% of the class was dumb. She wasn't about to allow those dummies to screw up her weekend. She knew they wouldn't have the correct answer to the question, so she raised her hand.

Instead of using their vocals to answer the teacher's question, students began coughing, whispering, and mumbling things she could barely understand.

Ughhh... I hate them. She thought. *I can't wait until graduation. I'm out this piece. I can bet my last breath none of them are going to walk across the stage. Hell, they probably could care less. But that's their dumb ass problem.*

"Fire away, Jazz." The teacher said.

"Four defense mechanisms are Pathological, Denial, Suppression, and Passive Aggressive Behavior."

The teacher smiled at Jazz; she then looked at the rest of the class,

"Because of Jazz you guys will have a stress-free weekend. Thank her."

"Fuck her." One girl yelled out.

Just then, the bell rang and the students made their way out of class. As Jazz walked off the school campus, she pulled out her Sidekick from her Coach Book bag and texted her cousin, Yay. She was letting her know that she would be at the burger stand on the corner by the school. When Yay-Yay felt like being bothered with Jazz, she would pick her up from school. They would either go shopping, compliments Jazz's mother, or go hang out at one of Yay-Yay's play date's house. This particular Friday, Yay's one and only best friend was out of town. And since Yay's scandalous ways caused her to have very few associates, she allowed Jazz in her space. You would think the fact that they were first cousins, as their mothers are sisters and them only being three years part ; Jazz is 17 and Yay is 20 they would be close. Jazz wished. Jazz would be lucky if Yay would even talk to her some days. And that would hurt her feelings. Jazz would never treat Yay badly, no matter how many times Yay would diss her and make her feel bad. She would brush it off and write it off as Yay being Yay-Yay. Everything Yay did, Jazz would make excuses for her. If she screwed one of her now ex-home girl's men, Jazz would say, he must have come on to her, and/ or took advantage of her because she was drunk. If she refused to mess with a dude who couldn't give her money, Jazz would say she was about her hustle and nothing in the world is free. Nobody could talk about Yay-Yay to Jazz, not even her best friend, Laurie, because she would get defensive; that's why people often talked about her too. For her to take up for somebody like Yay, they thought she had to be just like her. And the fact that her mother was known to sleep around didn't help. Although Jazz was far from Yay-Yay and nothing like her momma, people that didn't know her personally or just didn't like her because a lot of guys admired her pretty face, sassy attitude, and intelligence would say she was just as shady as her cousin and a hoe like her mother. Trust me when I say, that is far from true. Jazz never really tripped about what people said; she didn't have to prove who she was to nobody. Her motto is, "Only God Can Judge Me," but if she was in her "I'm not the one you wanna fuck with today" moods, she would check you quick. That didn't happen often; she tried to keep it ladylike at all times. Her grandmother always said, "You must carry yourself how you want to be viewed. If you respect yourself, so will others." But sometimes you gotta throw that lady shit out the window, and show assholes that you are not the one.   Jazz walked into the gate of the burger stand and got in line. She already knew what she wanted; a cheese burger special. She pulled her Sidekick back out of her bag and texted Yay letting her know that she had arrived at the burger stand. She then went on the web to mess around on FaceBook. Jazz's attention was taken away from responding to one of her friends messages when she heard a guy behind her speak.

"What's up girl?" He said.

She turned around and smiled. It was Peter, the guy that used to stay next door to Yay-Yay when he lived in the projects. Peter is also one of many guys that had a crush on Yay-Yay.

"What's up Peter; what are you doing up here?" Jazz asked.

"Handling some business."

She should have known. Pete and his homeboy, Ken, serve that West Coast Fire: known to some as ecstasy! Most of the high school kids were on it.

"Oh. Ok!" She said. She then looked around. "Yay coming up here." She spoke with excitement.

"So; what that mean? Is that your way of telling me that I can't give you a ride home?"

He looked her up and down seductively.

She blushed.

"I'm good. And why you wanna give me a ride; I thought you were checking my cousin?"

"Never that! I wanna know what's up with you?"

He lied, and half told the truth. Although the sexual attraction he held for Yay was still there, he wasn't about to push up on her and get dissed again. Besides that, Jazz had grown up to be a sexy little cutie.

I'll say. Jazz thought. She couldn't even finish enjoying the thought because of a hater.

"If you ain't no pimp, then the hoe don't want cha." said a hating ass tramp.

It was the same bald head, ugly bitch from 7th period. Jazz looked and rolled her eyes.

Does she not know hating makes her look uglier than what she already is...?

"Bitch, roll 'em again and I'll black 'em." The girl said walking her way.

"Y'all chill that out man. Why y'all hating? "Peter said in Jazz's defense.

Deonta's tall, bumpy face ass had the nerve to add in his two cents.

"Naw, P, you don't wanna mess with her. That trick's a hoe. You ain't heard? "

"Stale her out, y'all. That shit ain't cool." P said.

"Peter its cool." Jazz said.

Today was the day that she had to throw the lady shit out the window. She wasn't trying to get embarrassed in front of the guy that was flirting with her. It was time to turn the tables.

"Nigga, hoe or not, I wouldn't give your dusty ass no play if my life depended on it."

That was so unattractive of me. Why did I let them take me there? Oh well!

Bumpy face spoke up: "I'll slap you bitch, but it ain't worth it. I'll just let my home girl fuck you up."

Old boy was fronting. He knew damn well he wasn't about to do nothing to Jazz. If he had, all Jazz had to do was say one word, and the entire project would be on his head. Her daddy and uncle resting in peace are well respected in the same projects the big mouth boy stayed in.

"Don't front like you doing me a favor." She told him.

He didn't say a word. She then turned to the females, "All three of you BUM bitches are ugly. You couldn't be me on my worst day. Don't hate me because you are you and I'm me."

"Oh this bitch trying to show out." One girl said.

"She don't be talking that shit when we at school." Another girl said.

"I know you ain't trying to get smart with the homeboy." the first girl that spoke said.

Jazz responded by giving her the middle finger. The big, yellow, husky girl walked up on Jazz. She pointed her finger at her,

"I will beat your ass, little girl." she warned.

"I know one thing; you better get that finger out my face."

"And if I don't?" the girl said and thumped Jazz on the nose.

Without giving it a thought, Jazz gave her a right hook and then a quick left, and then another right. The girl could try all she wanted to grab Jazz's hair, but it wasn't happening; Jazz was too quick. Jazz mopped that ass; she dragged her, kicked her, and at one point, she bent down with her hand wrapped around the girl's hair and punched her a few times in the face. The school crowd was hype. Not one of the girl's friends tried to jump in and help. They were scary anyway; they only talked their mess because they thought they could bully Jazz.

"One Time." Someone yelled out, letting it be known that the police were near. Peter then grabbed Jazz, and Deonta grabbed the other girl. Deonta and the girl Jazz was fighting ran out of one side of the gate and Peter and Jazz ran out the other side to his car. He hit the alarm on his car unlocking the doors. Jazz hopped in on the passenger side. Peter was getting in on the driver's side when something told him to look up. He did, and that's when he saw a purple Camaro. He and the driver made eye contact. The driver frowned up her face, rolled her eyes and rolled up her window. Peter stood there for a second in shock. He couldn't help but shake his head.

"What you shaking your head for? I know I shouldn't have let that girl take me there." Jazz said when Peter got in the car.

He started to tell her that wasn't the reason he was shaking his head. He wanted to let her know that he was shaking his head at her cousin, he knew Yay had to see what went down, but went against it. He didn't want to start no mess.

"Sometimes the only way you will get respect is if you fight." Peter told her. *Or if you gain status,* he thought!

"Right!" She said just above a whisper.

The two pulled into traffic. Peter was about to ask her where she lived so he could take her home, but then thought that he wouldn't mind spending a little time with her. He looked over at Jazz.

"Would you like to make a few runs with me before I take you home?"

Jazz didn't respond. She was thinking about the fight. She then thought about Yay. *Oh shoot,* she thought, let me call her.

"Dammit. I left my bag." She said. "My phone and everything was in there."

"My bad. I saw your bag drop to the ground and I was meaning to pick it up, but I had to make sure you were alright. I was scared if I took my eyes off of you I wouldn't have been able to stop the fight if somebody jumped in. What was in it?"

"Nothing, but my phone, my wallet and a few notebooks. Can I use your phone to call my cousin?"

"My battery dead." he told her.

She asked did he have a car charger. He told her the fuse blew out the lighter. She sighed.

"I'll get you another phone, don't trip." Peter said.

"No, I'm good. My mom has insurance on it."

"Word? But you never answered my question."

Puzzled, she asked, "What question?"

"Ride with me a few places and then let's get something to eat."

"Sure." Jazz smiled.

After Peter made a few drops around Los Angeles County, he and Jazz decided to go to the Beverly Center, where they enjoyed a meal at the Grand Lux Cafe. Jazz could barely have a conversation with Peter because all the boy did was crack jokes. If he wasn't cracking jokes, he was telling her how pretty she was. Basically, her time spent with Peter was full of laughs and blushing. They did get serious for a good thirty minutes. That's when they talked about Peter's mom passing, how he went from a nobody to a somebody, and how he was looking for a nice young lady to accept him for him. Jazz talked about her father being in prison and how she was happy that he would be home within the next year. She told him about her dreams of becoming a famous tap dancer and that she couldn't wait until she graduated. Jazz not only wanted to get away from Locke, but she wanted to go to college. Her major would be dance of course. By the end of their evening together, the two agreed that they had a good time and wouldn't mind seeing each other again. Not wanting to speak to soon, and/ or seem desperate, Peter and Jazz kept their thoughts about how they imagined the other in their future to themselves. Jazz felt Peter was mature enough to respect a lady, plus he was cute to her and made her laugh. Peter felt that he finally found somebody that he could be his self with; goofy or silly Peter is what they used to call him back in the day. Some people still did. Jazz seemed as if she liked him for him and not his money or hell of a sex game. Sex and money is all the girls wanted him for; he knew eventually he would get tired of it, and when he did, he wanted someone like Jazz on his team.

****

The sun had set and the moon was coming out when Peter dropped Jazz off at home. As soon as she got in the house she told her mother what happened at school. She would wait until later to tell Pam about her date with Peter. Pam was going off about the fight. She was ready to go up there and whip some ass. Pam was a straight rider. She didn't take no mess, especially when it had something to do with Jazz. Jazz told her mother that she handled hers and that it was no need to go up there. She told her that she was sure they didn't want none after she put a beating on the biggest, loudest one from the crew. She also told her that since she was six months away from graduating, that if they did try something she would bring it to the counselor's attention. She didn't want to get kicked out or have a suspension on her record. Her mother told her that was cool, but promised if she ever saw any of them bitches she was going to tap that ass.

"Ok, mommy." Jazz said and went up to shower.

The entire time in the shower she thought about Peter. He was such a gentleman. He pulled her seat out for her, paid for the meal, and he even offered to get her a new cell phone. He showed interest in what was important to her. If she would have known that all she had to do was snag an older dude to spark her interest, she would have been dating. She then thought about Yay-Yay; the older dudes she hung around were only after one thing: sex. Peter was one of the most mature twenty-two year olds she met thus far. She prayed that Yay-Yay still felt the same way she felt about him when she dissed him back in the day.

After Jazz showered and put on her PJ's, she called Yay-Yay. When Yay answered the phone, she went off on Jazz about her not being at the school when she went up there, and how she wasn't answering her phone calls. Once Yay was finished venting, Jazz told her about the fight as if she did not know.

"Well you still should have called." Yay said.

"I lost my phone and Peter's phone was dead." She told her.

"Oh you was with Peter? Peter, Ken's Peter?" Yay played it off.

"Yes. But it's not like that. I know he's checking for you."

"Girl, please. That's all you. I don't like him. I'm trying to get with Ken."

Jazz was so excited.

"I'm going to set something up. Girl, when you wanna go? How about this weekend?" Jazz said all in one breath.

Yay ignored the excitement in her tone.

"That's fine."

"Alright, girl. I'm going to call Peter. But let me tell you about our date today."

"Um. Call Peter and let him know what's up. I got something to do. Tell me tomorrow what he said."

"K!" Jazz said.

Yay ended the call.

****

Jazz and Yay-Yay were at Jazz's house getting ready so they could go hook-up with Peter and Ken. The two cousins went shopping earlier that day. Jazz picked out what she thought was simple: a burnt orange stretch dress that complimented her dark brown skin tone. Jazz's small frame and round bottom made her look like a super model. She wore a pair of silver, Steve Madden sandals, and matching silver accessories set the outfit off just right. After Jazz applied her Moth To A Flame lip glass from Mac, she blotted her face with her walnut Bobbi Brown compact foundation. She turned to look at her older cousin. Yay wore her beauty with confidence. She looks hot: Jazz thought. Yay-Yay wore a black mini skirt with a red, backless shirt that showed her belly and some clear, 4 inch stilettos. She dressed her face with silver eye shadow and red lipstick. She looked like an off duty stripper - which she was.

Yay could see from the corner of her eyes that Jazz was admiring her sexiness. It wasn't nothing new; Jazz always did.

"You look pretty." Jazz told her cousin.

"I know." She simply replied.

"You think this looks right?" Jazz asked. Looking down at her outfit.

"You picked it out. I guess."

Before Jazz could say something negative about herself, her mother walked into the room and spoke,

"You look classy and beautiful." Her mother said.

"What about me, auntie?"

"Yay, you look sexy. Something someone your age can look."

"I wanna look sexy too."

Pam eyed her daughter.

"Just because you hang with a 20 year old don't mean you're grown. When you get Yay's age I may let you dress that sexy." She teased.

Pam never dictated what Jazz wore. She didn't have to. Jazz never liked to show too much. When Pam used to shop for her and buy her little shorts, she wouldn't wear them; she said it made her look fast. Maybe she learned it from her grandmother; her granny always said, showing too much don't make you look better, just slutty, and easy. Or maybe it was the fact that she didn't like the attention her mother received when she barely wore any clothes that Jazz was selective about how much she showed. But tonight she wanted to look just as slutty as Yay, if not sexier. It never really mattered before how she looked compared to Yay, because Yay would get all the attention anyway, and she was cool with that. But now that she had a guy's attention that she liked, she wanted to keep it and not allow Yay-Yay or anyone else to take the spotlight.

"I think I want to wear my skirt." Jazz said.

"Girl, please. It's time to go." Yay said and walked out the room like her word was final. It was, because Jazz kissed her mother and followed behind her. The girls walked out the door and jumped in Yay-Yay's Camaro en route to the west of L.A where Peter stayed.

****

When the girls pulled up in front of Peter's house, Jazz called him to let him know they were outside. Peter came out, unlocked his gate and escorted the girls into the house.

"Ain't this about a bitch." Yay thought, when she walked in the house and saw Ken with some Puerto Rican girl. She looked at Jazz who looked at Peter. Peter just hunched his shoulders as if he didn't know why Ken brought that girl over there. Jazz sensed her cousin's vibe. She was not happy at all. And neither was Jazz. That was not the plan.

"You ready?" Jazz asked, looking at Ken like he was her date and he dissed her for another girl.

No this stupid little girl did not just say that out loud, thought Yay.

"Ready for what we just got here, damn, relax girl. She said. She then looked at Ken;

"Hi Ken."

He looked at Yay, threw his head up as a way of saying what's up, and continued talking to his girl.

Jazz did not speak to him, she didn't know him like that, and plus she did not like his attitude. She could tell he thought he was all that.

"What y'all drinking?" Peter asked.

Jazz hunched her shoulders. Yay told him that she wanted brown. Jazz said her too. Peter walked over to the bar and made the girls their drinks.

"XO on the rocks." he announced as he handed them their drinks. He then rolled up a blunt and they enjoyed each other's company. Ken and his girl stayed to themselves.

"It's real fucked up when your own blood do you in. I guess when they said keep your grass cut low so you can see the snakes they weren't excluding family!"

Chapter 1

The Present

Higher than an eagle off that Kush, Peter and Kendrick sat on their front porch in a zone observing the festivities that took place on their block. Young girls were playing jump rope, middle school boys were slap boxing, trying to impress the girls who they assumed were watching. Cruising up the block sitting on gold D's and bumping Soldier Boy's latest hit, the hood ice cream truck was ready to supply its customers with everything from candy, ice cream, chili cheese chips and more. The aroma from the BBQ function up the block filled the two homeys' nostrils and broke them away from their thoughts.

"I'm cool on Big Twin's shit today. His baby momma forever coming through starting shit. Then she wanna call the police when he slap her ass. Aye, that Bar-B-Q do smell good, tho!"

When Ken didn't get an immediate response, he glanced over at Peter. He shook his head when he noticed who had Pete's attention. It was the young hoochie next door: Sabrina. She was getting dropped off in a white Chevy Impala SS a few houses down from her house by a dude who looked to be at least 18 years her senior. Sabrina was only fifteen, all the make-up she wore didn't make her look any older, but her banging ass body and the things she'd let a nigga do for some paper, made most dudes forget her age.

"Ho or not, she's only 15 nigga." Ken stressed.

"And? So what? Shit, I'm only 22. Besides, I ain't going to do nothing to her she ain't already had done." Peter responded, never taking his eyes off Sabrina.

Ken shook his head in disgust. Did his childhood friend have any morals?

"That's crazy. You'll put your dick in anything."

Once Sabrina was out of Peter's eyesight, meaning walking through her front door, Peter responded.

"That's not true. The only things I go in are warm holes and they gotta be attached to a female."

Shaking his head, Ken replied, "Yeah, whatever. You burnt my nigga."

"Call me what you want, but you won't call me a gay. If Yay-Yay crazy ass wasn't on her way, I would have hollered at shorty. I know she's waiting on me to say the word and she gon be ready. I see how she be checking for a nigga."

Ken cracked a half-smile. *This fool is unbelievable. That's my nigga, tho.*

"Don't you mean Jazz?

"Nope. Jazz is at dance practice. Yay-Yay on her way over, tho. You know she be acting all jealous when she sees a nigga talking to anybody else besides her or Jazz."

"You crazy. You don't think you playing it close?" Ken asked.

"Nope. Why you say that?"

"Why? 'Cuz, you already hitting your girl's relative, and now you trying to hit Sabrina's young ass. Nigga, Sabrina's right next door. I swear you playing with fire."

"I'm a man... A man with needs."

Ken cocked his head sideways and looked at Peter with a curious stare.

"Don't tell me Jazz still ain't gave you none?"

"Nope! She still talking that shit about waiting until she turns eighteen. I can respect that, but I gotta take care of me, you feel me?"

Kendrick laughed, "Well in that case, it is what it is. But you still a cold ass nigga."

"Pretty much." Peter agreed and licked his lips.

Just as the two finished their conversation, Yay-Yay's high yellow, bow legged, hooched out, sexy ass walked up.

"Hey Boo." She greeted, Peter. She then walked over and ran her hand through his curly hair. "What's up with you?"

She wants something. Peter thought. Yay ain't nice unless she has a reason.

"Chilling." Peter said.

Yay looked over at Ken. "What's up square." She said in a playful tone.

"Square? I got your square. Peter you better learn how to keep 'em in line."

Yay-Yay rolled her eyes; she then directed her attention back on Peter.

"Here" She said, tossing him a Swisher, and then a bag a purple haze. "Roll this. I'll be back. I hope you got some ice."

When she turned to walk in the house both Peter and Ken caught a glimpse of her ass.

"Damn." Peter mumbled.

Not my type. Ken thought to himself.

When Yay came back out of the house, she had a cup in her hand of Vodka and juice mixed. Sipping from the cup she eyed Peter seductively. Peter wasn't all that good looking: standing at an even six foot, mocha skin tone, with big brown eyes and natural curly hair you would think that was the reason he was a ladies man. Nope, like Yay, the females were attracted to how freely he gave his money, what he could do with his tongue, and the monster that hung between his legs. Yay's eyes followed Peter's hand as he passed Ken the blunt. Now he was the one that was fine to Yay. Ken is 6'2, unlike Peter, Ken has a nice build, dark as they come and wears his hair in a fade. Yay wished she could find out what he was working with. She always said if she ever got a chance to give Ken some, she would put it on him so good he would change his mind about fucking with girls of Yay's caliber. Ken claimed he didn't mess with girls who did not know the difference between acting like a lady and a ghetto diva. That day Jazz brought Yay to Peter's house in hopes of them hooking up, he damn near chocked on his soda laughing so hard when Peter begged him to chill with her. He already knew how Yay got down; the bitch was a ho.

"Please, please just for today" Peter begged.

"Hell fucking no. What I look like fucking with a stripper? Shit, being a stripper ain't half as bad as fucking with a gold digging hood rat, and she's both."

Peter kept on begging. So what Ken did to let him know he was serious: he called his Puerto Rican hottie from the valley over and chilled with her all up in Yay's face. Yay did not want to feel played, so she stayed and chilled. She had never been so aggravated and jealous, watching Jazz laugh off of all Peter's corny jokes, and Ken and his stuck-up bitch having a good time talking about whatever that was stupid. Like college and her week at work. *If I really wanted to, I can fuck either one of their niggas. Yay's ego told her.* And just like her ego said, she had Peter; he was wrapped around her finger. He paid her car note and kept money in her pockets. He was breaking her off at least five hundred a month on top of what she was making for selling X pills for him and Ken. Her ego told her, it *may take a little more work, but she would have Ken one day too.* We'll see!

After Ken was done hitting the blunt he passed it back to Peter. Yay jumped up from the window sill she was sitting on.

"Excuse you nigga. You gon' learn today on how to rotate somebody else's shit."

Kendrick ignored her. He wasn't tripping off nothing Yay-Yay was talking about. He did what he did on purpose. He simply didn't like the hood rat bitch.

"Peter, give me my shit." She said, and tried to take it out of his hand.

"Watch out." He said, moving his hand.

"Watch out my ass. Give me my shit. I ain't playing."

Peter looked her up and down slowly, he licked his lips.

"Let me give you a charge?" He told her.

Yay looked at Ken one last time, rolled her eyes, and then walked over to Peter and climbed on his lap. He stared at her perfect set of 38D cups and again licked his lips. The softness of her ass and the fact that she didn't wear any panties under that jean skirt had Peter extra hard. He slapped her on the ass.

"I'm going to fuck the shit out of you." He told her.

"I know." She replied.

Peter blew the ash off the blunt, and looked up at Yay-Yay while putting the lit end of the blunt in his mouth. Yay then leaned forward pressing her breast against his chest and placed her mouth on the other end of the blunt; it looked as if they were kissing.

This nigga Peter is a fool. I wonder if he really likes this bitch.

Kendrick's thoughts where interrupted when the dark-brown complexion cutie walked up. Jazz looked like Kelly Rowland from Destiny Child, but a little shorter with a nicer frame. Ken hit Peter on the leg,

"Here come Jazz", he mumbled.

Peter wanted to push Yay-Yay off of him, but that would make him look guilty. So he didn't stop with the charge until Yay-Yay's lungs couldn't take any more of the Kush smoke, which was about a second after Jazz walked onto the porch.

Hands on hips, Jazz snapped,

"Yalonda, what are you doing sitting on my man like that, and Peter what the hell are you doing with your hands on her ass?"

Yalanda was pissed off when she heard her cousin's voice.

What the fuck was she doing over so early? This bitch always fucking some shit up. She thought.

After coughing out her lungs she answered Jazz with a question,

"Why aren't you at dance practice?"

She got up off Peter's lap. She then coughed some more. When she was done, she asked another question,

"And what it look like? He was giving me a charge!"

She picked up her drink and took a sip from it and went back and sat on the tip of the window sill.

"What I tell you about acting so jealous? Yay-Yay's family, man." Peter said.

Jazz looked over at her pretty cousin and gave a weak smile.

"Okayyyyy. Don't nobody want Peter but your ass." Yay-Yay lied.

Jazz ignored her comment. Instead, she acknowledged Ken who just stared straight ahead.

"Hey, Ken. How are you?"

"What's up, Jazz?" He said, getting up.

He was ready to bounce being around the trio. Peter, Yay-Yay, and Jazz aggravated the fuck out of him. For one, Yay and Pete were scandalous, and for two, Jazz was dumb as hell. How in the fuck she can't see the two are making a fool of her?

"Alright, homey, get at me. I'm about to have Yay make a few drops."

"Where?" Kendrick replied.

"Them niggas in Pasadena want some, some niggas on the Eastside of LA, and some bitches she know in Watts. And then the regular at the club."

Ken nodded his head as if he was agreeing, walked off the porch, hopped in his Lexus and rolled off. He needed to go check on his mother. She recently found out his father was cheating and she had been flipping ever since. Ken was meaning to get at Pete about him and his mother leaving to go out of town to stay with her sister for a while; maybe while he was out there helping his moms get settled in he could set up shop , and expand their business, but it slipped his mind. Blame it on the weed.

Kendrick and Peter were hustlers on the rise. They were clocking, just them two by selling X pills; ones that they made themselves. If the two would have used their brain and went to college and studied medicine, they could have easily made money from the government or some non-profit organization with a legit gig. I guess it's true what they say, people can be so smart their actions prove their really stupid. Maybe not; at the rate they were going and the plans Kendrick had, they would probably be making more money than those clowns on Wall Street. If they didn't sleep on them heartless ass triplets: Grimy, Salty, and Envious.

"Come give your man a kiss." Peter told Jazz.

She smiled, walked over and kissed her baby on the lips. She loved his funny looking self and he loved her pretty ass. No matter how much he cheated on her, no one could take Jazz's place. She was one-of-a-kind. The other broads he dealt with were just a fuck. As he kissed Jazz, he rubbed his hand from the center of her back and stopped right before he touched her behind. That part right there pissed Yay-Yay off. In her eyes he gave Jazz too much respect. He treated Jazz like she was a princess or some shit. *That bitch think she hot shit. Only if she knew.* Yay-Yay thought.

Peter whispered in Jazz's ear. Before she went in the house to wait on Peter in his room, like she was asked, she turned toward Yay-Yay.

"Be careful out there; k?"

 Jazz was sincere; she loved her cousin even if Yay acted like she hated her.

"Bitch I'm good dang. I know what the fuck I'm doing; that's why Peter has me on his team."

"I know Yay-Yay; I just be worried about you. You drinking and already high, you gotta be careful."

Yay stood up.

"Peter tell your girl that you got a thorough bitch to handle what she can't."

This bitch always trying to start some shit. That's what good dick will do to you. Peter thought.

"What the hell does that mean? " Jazz asked defensively.

"Sometimes I think I'm auntie's daughter. She gets hers like I get mine. We don't wait on nobody to give us shit. I tell you about fake bitches."

"Well that's a pretty fucked up thing to say. Because I chose not to risk my life by doing illegal things I'm a fake? What the hell ever, Yalanda."

"Come on y'all cut that out." Peter intervened.

"Say no more." Jazz said, walking into the house and slamming the door behind her.

She couldn't understand why her cousin always threw salt at her.

Peter looked at Yay-Yay;

"You always starting shit. Come and get this shit."

Yay licked her tongue out at him and followed him in the house.

"Wait in the den." Peter told Yay-Yay. "I'll be right back let me check on her."

Peter walked in the room and checked on Jazz; she was laid across the bed turning the channel and talking on the phone. He climbed onto the bed; she opened her legs allowing him to rest there. Then with his tongue he began licking on her belly ring. Jazz knew what was about to go down, and no way did she want Laurie, her good friend to hear.

"Laurie I'll call you back. My boo wants some attention. I promise I will be at practice tomorrow. I just missed my boo this weekend and I had to see him. Don't whatever me. Now bye." Jazz ended the call.

She sat her cell next to her on the bed. She then began to rub in Peter's curly hair. Moaning softly as he licked her belly button, he worked his way up to her breast. She pulled his head up and kissed him.

"I love you babe", She whispered.

"I love you too." He said.

Peter was hard as a rock.

"Take off your clothes."

Jazz got up and took her clothes off. Peter stared at Jazz's perfect body. He licked his lips.

"I can't wait to make love to you." Peter told her.

"Two months, only two months and I'm all yours." She said with a smile.

Jazz lay on the bed with her legs open waiting for Peter to take her to another world. She wouldn't allow Peter to make love to her, she promised herself that she would wait until she was at least eighteen, but that didn't stop her from allowing Peter to pleasure her with his tongue. It was his idea, and when she finally gave in, she was glad she did. He licked her in spots that her fingers never found and she was convinced that it was okay. It had to be oaky because that shit felt good as hell. Peter had been pleasuring Jazz for three months and she loved it. Like always, Jazz was either in another zone once Peter got her to her climax or she was fast asleep. Luckily, this time she was fast asleep because Peter had a nut to bust.

****

Meeting in the next room

Peter pushed Yay-Yay toward the couch roughly, "turn around and bend over." He told her. She did. He then lifted up her skirt.

"You got a pretty ass." He said, rubbing on her ass and kissing on her neck.

Why can't I resist this nigga? Yay-Yay thought as she felt her body yearning to feel Peter inside of her. *Because of the money and the dick; yes, that's it!*

 Peter rubbed his hard pipe up and down Yay-Yay's clit ready to enter.

"Damn you wet. You want this dick don't you?"

"Mmmmm hummm…." Yay moaned.

Peter quickly entered in Yay-Yay's warm volt and they both let out a moan.

"Shh…." Peter said as he covered Yay-Yay's mouth.

He knew it was feeling good to her like it was to him, and he liked when she moaned, but he be damned if he let Jazz hear.

"This is some good pussy." Peter whispered as he banged Yay-Yay from the back.

Yay-Yay began contracting her muscles, she knew Peter couldn't take it when she did that, and would normally call her name in pleasure. And that's what she wanted. But she was fooled this time; that nigga was scared that he would wake Jazz up. Instead, he sucked on her neck, making a hickey, and pumped faster and faster until he nutted all in her. They both collapsed on the couch. Normally after a good fuck they would chill and smoke, but of course this time they couldn't because Jazz was in the other room, plus Yay-Yay had work to do. Peter got up, pulled up his pants, went to his stash, came back and handed Yay-Yay 500 X pills to deliver.

"Call Kendrick when you're done; he'll either meet you, or come pick up the money."

"Why because you and Jazz going to be kicking it tonight?" she said with an attitude.

"Man, be quiet." He said, he then kissed her on the mouth and walked toward the door. That was her cue to shake the spot. She held her hand out. Peter shook his head, went in his pockets, and like always broke Yay-Yay off.

"Thanks." She said, as she walked toward door.

"For what?" He wanted his ego struck.

"The money and the nut." She said and walked out the house.

Once Yay-Yay was gone, Peter went in the bathroom, took a shower and went to go cuddle with Jazz.

Flashback

Three months ago

Peter, Kendrick, and a few of their homeboys from their Car Club were hanging in the parking lot of the skating rink. Skate Depot in Cerritos was the spot. That's where the dudes would go: mostly car clubs to show off their rides, see who played the loudest music, dressed the best, and picked up the most females. The gold diggers hoped to get picked up by a nigga with some dollars. That's the only reason Yay-Yay hung out there. Besides getting money and looking good; fine ass niggas was the reason she enjoyed life. Anyway, Yay was chilling the entire night, never tripping off Peter or Kendrick who she had noticed earlier that day. For one, she didn't like Ken because he dissed her, second, Peter was stuck on her little cousin now that she didn't want him, and lastly, there were plenty of other dudes out there that Yay was interested in. Peter couldn't help it, he tried to ignore her, but he couldn't; Yay was just so damn sexy to him. He watched her damn near all night. Yay caught him a few times staring, but didn't trip; she was used to it. It wasn't until she smelled the Kush aroma coming from Peter's direction that she decided to make her way over there.

"What's up y'all?" She said to the crowd that was standing with Peter.

Everybody spoke but Kendrick. He continued talking to the shorty that was with him.

"What up, Yay, you wanna hit this?" Peter said offering Yay the blunt.

Once she took the blunt from his hands, he then made small talk with her.

"What you doing up here?" Peter asked.

"Chilling like everybody else." She replied.

"Who you with?"

"My home girl, Paris."

"The one that work at the club with you?"

"Yeah, Peter, you know P works at the club."

"Oh. What you got going for tomorrow?"

"Damn, can I get through with today? What's up with all these questions? I can't even get high good."

"My bad."

Silence.......

"Why you didn't go to the Bahamas with Jazz and her momma?"

Yay was about to snap on his ass, but the question threw her off.

"The Bahamas?"

"You didn't know? It was a graduation gift from her father."

Yay was heated in the inside, but she played it off.

"I thought they were going to Jamaica. They went to the Bahamas?" Was the only thing she could think of to say.

Silence.....

"You alright?" He asked.

"I'm good."

All the time she was thinking in her mind how dirty Jazz and her aunt were for not inviting her. Her aunt knew that her own mother would never spend any time with her or take her any place, they didn't get along and plus her mother has a pill addiction that takes all her money. Since Yay could remember, ever where she went...Amusement parks, Las Vegas, Atlanta, Walt Disney World she, her aunt, and when Jazz's father was out, they all did those things together like a family. Secretly, she was heartbroken and wondered why they left her out. She thought about not talking to Jazz for a good while. Well, until she needed something. Her not talking to Jazz was the reason she missed out on the trip. Jazz had called her for a week straight and Yay never returned her call, so she invited her best friend, Laurie. Although it was Yay-Yay's fault that she missed the trip, Jazz would still have to pay for it. She wanted revenge.

"What are you smiling at?" Peter asked Yay.

"I'm high, that's all. I always smile when I am high."

She was smiling because she came up with the perfect idea and Peter was going to help it play out. She would hook Peter up with her friend Paris, and she would get another chance at getting at Ken. So that night she and her friend Paris told Peter it would be a grand idea that the four of them went back to his house, but Kendrick declined; that left the three of them.

When they got to Peter's the girls took off their shoes and made themselves comfortable, per, Peter's request. After their first drink, Paris asked Peter could she buy a pill from him. Just like they knew he would, Peter said that she didn't have to buy it.

"Y'all company. Whatever y'all want it's on me.", were his exact words.

That was all she wrote. They had drinks, weed, and Peter and Paris popped at least two pills that night. Peter even ordered Denny's to go. They chilled and kicked it until Yay's plan went into motion. Paris seduced Peter, which wasn't hard to do. He already told the girls that Jazz wasn't giving him none. They used that to their advantage. After Paris' lap dances she could see Peter's erection through his pants. "Let me help with that," she said and dropped to her knees, pulled out his rock hard pipe, and put it in her mouth. He was in La La Land. Watching Paris suck off Peter turned Yay-Yay on and she decided to join. Yay started her foreplay with Paris. She sucked on her breast and played with her hotbox. Paris and Yay switched positions; Paris was licking Yay's juices while Yay blew on Peter's balls. Peter loved that because that's who he wanted anyway. Once the foreplay was over, the three freaked on each other all night. Peter couldn't wait to show Ken the tape he secretly made of him having the time of his life.

The next morning they woke up to breakfast in bed and a fat blunt. After Paris ate breakfast she had to run. Her babysitter needed her to pick up her baby. Peter called a cab for her. Yay stayed; Peter had offered to take her shopping and a trip to Catalina if she did. The nigga was a trick. For Yay, he was just what the doctor ordered. When her and Peter's weekend was over, Yay was in love with her cousin's man' sex game and his fat pockets. Peter was in love with the fact that he was able to suck, fuck and spend time with one of the baddest bitches in L.A. It didn't take long before Yay was spoiled by Peter. She even began to have a little feelings for him. She would get jealous if he would flirt with his other workers and she hated the way he treated Jazz like she was a princess. Peter was feeling her too but not to a point where he wanted to wife her or nothing like that. She was a fine bitch to fuck, chill, and work with. But the shit was getting out of hand, Yay was being too bossy. She was beginning to act like she owned him, and it started to seem as if she didn't care that Jazz found out. He had to cut the tramp off soon. But did he have the willpower?

"What's done in the dark shall come to the light."

Chapter 2

The sun peeped into her blinds and chirps from the birds that sat in the big oak tree by her window sang their famous happy melody; this was mother nature's way of letting Jazz know that she was blessed to live another day. "Wake up beautiful it's time for school." Jazz's pink, talking alarm clock repeated twice before she reached over and pushed snooze. She lay there for a few more minutes before she rose to sit up in her full size canopy bed. She looked up to the heavens, "Thank you, Jesus, for keeping my mommy safe last night." Jazz knew it was the grace of God that saved her mother from the dangerous lifestyle in which she lived. She learned that God was almighty by going to church with her grandmother on Sundays. Unlike her mother, Jazz knows God is the reason. Pam, her mom, just thought she was a bitch that couldn't be touched and that was the reason she was able to live the life in which she lived. Jazz hoped that one day her mother would realize that prayer is the reason she was kept another night from facing a tragic ending.

It was about 9:00pm when Jazz came home from her friend's house. Her mother and her date for the night were just leaving. Normally, Pam would meet her sponsors at the location they chose to handle their dealing, but her car was being serviced and she had no other choice; Pam wasn't missing any money. Jazz was two months shy of turning eighteen, which meant surprise party, and that was going to cost money. She goes all out for her baby girl. And then there was the payment due at the dance school Jazz attends. Not to mention her other monthly bills. Her husband, Jazz's daddy, is in jail; he sends money for the mortgage every month, but that's it. He has been tripping ever since his mother told him she saw Pam leaving from a hotel room with a man. Pam didn't see her that day, but she did see her the next day when she was checking in with another dude. Her mother-in-law was staying at the hotel for some church convention. Since then, every time she asks him for money, he tells her to get it from the niggas she's fucking, so she does. He wasn't talking that shit when she had to do what she did to save his life. She has to live with that night for the rest of her life.

"Hey, baby." Pam said to Jazz as she and her John were heading out the door.

"Hey." Jazz was dry. She knew the man that her mother was with was nothing more than some loser who probably was married and was paying for a peace of another woman's cookie. Pam ignored her daughter's vibe. She knew Jazz felt some kind of way about the different men she saw her with all the time. She knew her daughter wasn't stupid and knew that Pam was just messing with the dudes for money.

"Your dinner is in the microwave. And your dessert is in the freezer. I'll be back in a few hours." Pam said, "I love you."

"Love you too, mommy." Jazz said sincerely.

Jazz threw her book bag on the floor and ran to the bathroom trying to make it to the toilet; she had held her bladder for more than twelve hours before it gave in on the bathroom floor. She hated public restrooms. There's only a few people's bathroom she will use.

"You have a beautiful daughter. She looks just like you." Pam's sponsor complimented.

Pam turned to him and gave him a look that could scare the baddest mofo in Watts.

"Don't ever look at her again."

The sponsor threw his hands up to surrender. "I didn't mean anything by it."

Pam rolled her eyes and waited for him to open her car door. Just as the sponsor opened the door and Pam went to get in the car, the two froze.

There was a middle age black lady pointing a gun at Pam. She was trembling as tears rolled down her eyes.

"I should kill you bitch. You fucking home wrecker. Whore," The upset woman cried.

She then looked at the spooked man that was standing next to Pam.

"Does your wife know your trickling on this ghetto bitch?"

The man looked down at his wedding ring and shook his head no.

"That's what I figured. Call her now and tell her." The woman demanded.

She could see the hesitation in the man's eyes and that pissed her off even more.

"I said call her now. She has a right to know she is married to a dirty dick pussy hound."

Who does this bitch thinks she is? Pam thought. Yeah she did sleep with a few men for money and yes most were involved with someone, but she wasn't. Her husband is in jail. So, whatever problem that the woman had, she needed to take up with the one she married, not her.

"If you know what's good for you, you'll put that gun down and run to your car and get out of here as fast as you can." Pam warned.

She was so calm she scared the woman and she was the one holding the gun.

"Fuck you." The woman shot back.

"No bitch. Fuck you." Pam said walking up on her.

Her sponsor touched her arm. "Pam", he said in a whisper.

Pam jerked away from him and continued to walk up on the woman. The woman warned,

"One more step I'll shoot your ass."

Pam could tell the woman was nervous and she used it to her advantage.

"You know you fucked up right?" Pam said.

The woman looked in disbelief. She didn't expect her to be so bold. What she thought was that she would just come over, scare Pam and then deliver the most horrific news a living being would ever hear, and hope that the news would affect Pam like it did her.

"You make a bad name for women like me." The woman said.

"Let me tell you something." Pam was now up on the woman and poking her finger in her face.

"Let me explain something to you. Your husband comes to me for pussy; I don't call him and beg for dick. Although, he's probably one of the ones I like fucking. I don't know. But I know for a fact that he's a paying client. This pussy ain't for free."

Pam smirked when she read sorrow in the woman's eyes. That's what the bitch gets; she should have never brought her ass over here. Pam continued,

"Your husband was just business. I wanted nothing more than the half stack he spent on five hours of my time. He pays me to do what you don't do. Shit I don't mind."

Pam had no idea who her husband was. She had plenty of sponsors.

There's the owner of Chump Change production, the owner of T&T Auto Sales, the big time dope dealer in Long Beach, the guy that retired from the city, and the one she was with tonight; and each one was involved with someone, she didn't care. Their mate should be taking care of home.

She continued as she looked at the woman with disgust,

"Was you that fat and out of shape when he first met you? I bet you promised him that you would fulfill his every need, so why don't you swallow when he fucks you in the mouth? Why can't you women get up and take that shit when he wants some ass? And don't tell me you're not curious as to what it would feel like to get your pussy ate by another woman. You do love him and want him to be happy right? You want him to include you in everything right?"

The woman couldn't believe the bitch had the nerve to talk shit to her about what she did and didn't do. She couldn't believe that she was telling her about her husband.

"Bitch you're no fucking counselor; you're a home wrecker," she yelled and closed her eyes and fired.

Luckily, Pam had knocked her arm out the way before she pulled the trigger causing her .22 to fall to the ground. Pam punched her in the jaw so hard her head flew back. She then hit her with a cold left and her head flew to the side. Bam. She kicked her in the midsection. The woman hunched over in pain. Pam went to kick her again but the woman grabbed her leg, causing Pam to fall back. The woman got on top of her blood dripping from her mouth. She snatched her blade out of her ponytail. Breathing heavily she looked Pam in the eyes and spoke,

"Fuck letting you die from AIDS; I'm going to kill you myself..." She then smiled looking at the fear in Pam's eyes. Little did she know Pam was more scared of getting cut with the blade than dying from AIDS. It's been a long time coming.......

"Get the fuck off my momma." Jazz said, and then with all her might she snatched the woman by the hair, giving Pam the opportunity to toss the big bitch off her and get up off the ground. When Pam was up, she kicked the lady in the side of the face causing her to black out. Pam took the women's gun from Jazz and the two walked toward the house.

"I love you, baby. Mommy's sorry."

The woman laid there crying,

"It's because of you I had to abort my baby. I didn't want it to be born with AIDS. Now I have to leave my only son in this fucked up world alone. You destroyed my family. I swear you will pay from this."

Pam stopped in her tracks. And before Pam could muster up a thought the woman shouted,

"You're a selfish bitch, what will your daughter do when you die from being a slut?"

Without looking back Pam replied,

"Bitch you got five minute to get off my property. Try me if you want to."

After Jazz finished praying and thanking God for the ones he blessed her with, she went into her closet and picked out an outfit. Today she was wearing a pair of 7 For All Man Kind jeans and a white tank top. She then packed her bag for what she would wear to dance, which was a pair of stretch pants and a halter top. Once Jazz had everything together, she went into her bathroom and took a shower. She was meeting Laurie at Cal State L.A. Today was orientation.

Thirty minutes later, Jazz was walking into the kitchen with her mother.

"Hey, sweetie." Pam said to Jazz upon her entering the kitchen.

"Good morning, mom." Jazz replied.

"Jazz, I thank you for last night. But next time stay out of it. You could have gotten yourself hurt."

Pam's eyes began to water thinking about losing her only reason for wanting to live life to the fullest. It has been so many times that Pam wanted to give up on life, but when Jazz came to mind she knew she was needed in this world. She knew Jazz only wanted to help, but she couldn't have that. It was her job to protect her. Not the other way around.

"And you couldn't have? Mommy you risk your life everyday by doing what you do. Mom these men have girlfriends and wives. What if you get a stalker? No, what if you have AIDS?"

Pam's heart dropped. She wished all night that Jazz hadn't heard that part.

"Mommy, you say you love dad. Then love just him. You have to leave all these different men alone."

Pam was saved by the horn from the cab notifying them that he had arrived. Both Jazz and her mother gathered their things and headed out the door to the awaiting cab. When they got in front of the school, Jazz kissed her mother on the cheek, and before exiting the car she asked her to promise to take an AIDS test. Pam told her after she picked up her truck from the shop her next stop would be the doctor's office. That put a hopeful smile on Jazz's face. When the test came back clear, Jazz would ask her again to leave the men alone.

Chapter 3

Orientation was over; it went well. Jazz, Laurie and a few other girls they went to high school with decided that was the school for them. They couldn't wait to start and enjoy the college life. Jazz lingered behind talking to two girls she knew, while Laurie walked ahead. Her brother had called and told her he was driving around looking for her. When she spotted his Benz she called out to Jazz.

"Hurry up, girl." Jazz, was talking to some of their other friends in the campus parking lot. Jazz said her goodbyes to the two girls she was talking to and ran to catch up with Laurie.

"Girl my impatient brother is taking us to practice. My momma got caught up at work." Laurie informed her.

"No problem girl I'm glad you called me, I didn't feel like hearing what they were talking about. They forever got Yay's name in their mouths."

"What was they saying, girl?"

Jazz debated if she should tell Laurie or not, she knew if she did Laurie's mouth would get a little loose. Laurie couldn't stand Yay and Yay didn't care for her either. Laurie looked at Jazz from the corner of her eyes.

"I already know Yay-Yay is a ho. So you don't have to tell me that part."

"Don't start." Jazz pleaded with Laurie.

"I'm not. That's your cousin. I don't have to deal with her shady ass, but you do. I guess."

Jazz didn't respond.

The girls approached the Mercedes, and Diesel, Laurie's brother, got out to open their doors. He first opened the back passenger seat of the car door and Laurie got in. He then opened the driver back door and Jazz got in. Once they both were in, Jazz and Laurie looked at each other.

Who is the white girl? They thought.

 Diesel caught their expression and smiled exposing his deep dimples. Diesel looked in his rear view mirror as if reading the ladies' minds, he spoke.

"Ladies this is my new friend, Savanna." He smiled at the two and they smiled back. Both girls spoke and so did Savanna.

"Did you guys meet at school?" Laurie asked.

"No, I met him on my job." Savanna replied.

"Stop being nosey, momma," Diesel teased.

He turned the radio up. He knew his nosey little sisters' next question would be where she worked, and the silly chick probably would have told them a strip club.

Diesel is twenty years old; he attends USC on a full basketball scholarship. Word is he may be drafted before he finishes school. He'll find out in a few months. He and Laurie are also the children of the late Bones, a famous Jazz player who was killed in a car accident. Their father's insurance money and royalties left them more paid than they already are. The Kenslow family always had money; their mother is a big time attorney. However, she doesn't spoil the kids like Bones used to do. She made them work for what they wanted. Unlike most rich parents, she taught her kids the value of a dollar. Yeah they had maids and lived in a mansion over in Ladera Heights but they were far from the spoiled rich brats that Diesel chose to hang with. His mother couldn't stand the kids D hung with; if their parents ran out of money they were destined for failure. D really didn't like them either, but they were the only ones that accepted him for what he is: a handsome, blue eyed, biracial dude with money. People often said he looked like a mixed Justin Timberlake and had a body like Tyson Beckford. The girls love him, and jocks and the other dudes in his circle praise him. For one, he had skills on the court that kept their school winning ball games, and for two, it was because of him all the fine, sexy, and unattractive girls came around. Diesel is single and plans on staying that way. Thanks to his ex, Shannon; she left him for his once best friend. He promised himself that he would never mess with another black girl; she could be mixed, but not fully black. With the exception of his mother, he thought black girls were scandalous. He wasn't trying to get serious with anyone anyway; he's too young to settle down. He was a fool for trying the first time, now he's about to get drafted; he was good. So why was he secretly admiring Jazz? It was just something about her that turned him on. Was it her sassy, but intelligent talk? Was it her perfect coke bottle frame? Was it the way she carried herself, sweet and neat, or was it the fact that she never paid him any attention? Most of his sister's friends stayed in his face; they seem as if they only befriended his sister to get close to him. Not jazz; she was different.

That girl ain't no more than sixteen or seventeen. Plus she's my sister's friend. He thought as he held the door open for Jazz to exit the car. *But damn she's fine, an innocent fine.*

"Thanks D for the ride." Jazz said and walked toward the studio.

"You're welcome." He called out behind her.

It was the smile in his voice that made Jazz turn around and smile one more time at him before entering the doors of the studio. Laurie felt the vibe but kept it to herself. It was innocent flirting she assumed.

The entire ride to Savanna's apartment, Diesel was thinking about Jazz's young ass.

"Thanks for a good time." Diesel told Savanna as they pulled up in front of her place.

He had met her early that morning at an after hour. One thing lead to another and they ended up getting their freak on. He would have been dropped her off, but he had an emergency meeting at the college and after he had to pick up Laurie from orientation.

"You're welcome. I hope this won't be the last time I see you."

Diesel smiled.

"Nah, I'll be back up there real soon. As a matter of fact, my boy's leaving to go play football in Arizona in a few weeks. We're giving him a going away party. Gather some of the girls from the club and come do the party."

She didn't have anybody to do the party with, she didn't fuck with none of the bitches at the club, and the one friend that she had was dead. But she wouldn't tell him that. She was trying to see him as much as possible. There where dollar signs written all over him. She was going to find somebody to do the party with her.

"Alright just let me know. I still hope you use my number before then."

She got out the car and headed for the house. Diesel pulled off, heading back to the dance studio with Jazz on his mind.

Normally when Diesel had to pick his sister up from dance he'd either come back when it was over or wait in the car. Not today, he decided to go inside to watch Laurie and her friend do their thing. Damn she's good, Diesel thought as he watched Jazz lead the group. The way she moved her body to the beat and the moves she mastered, she could easily become the most desired choreography in the industry. Debbie Allen's studio housed some great dancers, but Jazz was beyond hot; she was bad. One of the dance instructors noticed Diesel and went over to introduce herself. She knew who he was, Laurie's fine ass brother but he didn't know who she was. She was the Latin cutie that could make him love again. Laurie told her all about the girl that broke his heart.

"Hey, guy." She said stealing Diesel's attention from Jazz.

"Hey, yourself." Diesel replied eying the physically fit but not too cute admirer.

· ·

****

Pam could not stop thinking about the lady confronting her about giving her and her husband AIDS. *Who the fuck was the bitch?* Pam thought. *Did the bitch follow me, how did she know where I lived?* Why would she assume I gave it to him? Pam didn't get that part. Pam looked at the clock on her Infinity truck. Jazz would be coming out any minute. She had to pull herself together. She went in her purse, pulled out a pill bottle, took a piece a paper out of her glove compartment, and poured a little of the white product on it and sniffed it all in two sniffs. She leaned her head back and let the product do what it was supposed to do: erase problems. Since the product was pure, meaning uncut, it only took a few minutes for it to take effect. Pam lifted her head up just in time to see Jazz saying her goodbyes to Laurie. She smiled at the guy who couldn't take his eyes off Jazz. *Look at my baby flirting*, she thought as she watched Jazz smile and wave bye to Diesel, and then she had the nerve to put on a cold walk. She gets it from her mommy, Pam said aloud.

"Hi, beautiful." Was the way Pam greeted Jazz.

"Hi, mommy." Jazz replied, and shut the door.

Pam couldn't pull off good before Jazz hit her with the question...

Jazz wanted to know if she had taken the AIDS test, she told her that she did and the results would be back in 72hrs. She also insured her that she wasn't infected. *When will I ever get the guts to tell her the truth*?

Pam looked over at her daughter; she could see worry written all over her face. She had to cheer her up.

"You feel like shopping?"

Jazz's eyes got big and so did her smile.

"Of course, diva." She said.

They both laughed.

"Divas rolling." Pam cheered as they pulled off en route to the South Coast Plaza.

******

A few hours later

Jazz and Pam where leaving out the mall when her cell phone began to sing Soldier by Destiny's Child. Her hands were full of bags so she couldn't answer it.

"Yay-Yay is going to be mad that we went shopping and didn't tell her. Pam said.

"How you know that's Yay-Yay?"

"The ring tone, duh!"

"You think you know our life?" Jazz teased and they both laughed.

By the time the two reached Pam's car and put the bags into the trunk, Jazz's cell rang again; it was Yay-Yay again. This time Jazz was able to answer.

"What, chick?" Is how she greeted Yay-Yay.

"Bitch where you at? You come the fuck to Peter's house now!"

"What's up? I'm with my momma; what happened?"

Pam looked at Jazz. She wondered what drama her niece had going on today. Yay was always getting herself into some mess and just like her momma; who called on Pam to help her out of a bind. Yay called on Jazz. Yay-Yay was going on and on about some bitch being over Peter's house talking shit. And how she believed she was fucking Peter; that's all Jazz needed to hear.

"Peter's house." She told her mother.

What bitches Peter got over here now? Jazz thought. *If it ain't one thing it's another.*

"What happened?" Pam's question pulled Jazz away from her thoughts.

Jazz sighed.

"Yay say some females over Peter's starting ish and that she think one's messing with Peter."

"Hmmm" was all Pam said.

She kept her thoughts about Peter and Yay to herself. She hated to admit that Yay was like her mother. Yay's mother was always in competition with Pam. Always trying to outdo her, she swore her sister invented Puncha nella 47: "*Whatever you can do, I can do or get better.*" Pam could see Yay was carrying some of the same traits. When would the cycle end?

When Jazz and Pam pulled up they saw Yay-Yay, Peter, and a light skin girl standing in the yard. Ken was standing on the porch. Pam walked on the porch and sat next to him.

"What's going on Yay?" Jazz asked as she approached the trio.

"This bitch right here being disrespectful." Yay screamed while pointing at the girl.

"Bitch, being disrespectful, you're the one over here up in me and my dude's business."

"Dude." Jazz said looking at the girl like she carried a disease. She then turned to Peter.

"What she mean dude?"

Peter was aggravated,

"Why don't you ask her, she right here?"

Jazz walked up on him. "No I'm asking you?"

"It's a figure of speech. Everybody knows that."

Peter was telling the truth. Girls on the Eastside called their homeboys their dude and home girls their girl.

"This dumb bitch," Kendrick was referring to Yay-Yay, "is fucking up our money".

He looked at Pam to see if she heard him disrespect her niece; she did but she let it go, she wanted to see how it was going to play out. Kendrick walked off the porch and over to the four.

"I wasn't going to say nothing; I thought you could handle it Pete, but I guess you can't so I'm going to handle this." He said. "First off Yay-Yay, you don't run this man or nothing he does. And when it comes to business you just do what we pay you to do, nothing extra. You don't dictate shit. "

He looked at Peter who was standing with his arms crossed.

This nigga was soft when it came to keeping bitches in line, but swore he was hard. Kendrick thought. *He gotta stop flirting so much... Hell naw, what he needs to do is leave Yay-Yay dumb ass alone if he can't check the bitch.* Looking back at Yay-Yay he continued, "When you come over here with all this nonsense you not only fuck up our clientele, you draw unwanted attention. You start shit that shouldn't be started."

He looked back at Pam and shook his head.

"You got your aunt over here and Jazz over on some shit that has nothing to do with you."

Yay knew he was right. But she would never admit it. She was jealous that Peter was flirting with the girl; he did every time she came by and he even gave her extra pills for free. Peter was a ho and if she let him they would have fucked. She wasn't about to let another bitch mess with her money. Niggas get new pussy and forget about the old.

"Kendrick you need to shut up." Yay-Yay said, "That's your homeboy so of course you are going to make like he was in the right. Peter won't you tell Jazz why you asked her to step in your office. Everybody knows your office is your bedroom."

In unison Ken and the girl was like, "Shut the fuck up."

Yay -Yay threw her hands in the air.

"What y'all wanna do?" she tested.

Yay wasn't no fighter. She only bluffed when Jazz or her other friends were around.

"On my momma, you got one more time and it's a wrap. Pete go get her work."

"Oh so you threatening to fire me?"

"You heard what I said." Ken was stern.

The yard was silent. Jazz felt like a fool. Pam was embarrassed for both her daughter and niece. The girl Yay accused Peter of was through with the whole situation, and Ken hated a scene. Peter came back out the house, handed the girl her work. Ken and the girl walked out the yard together, but went their separate ways. Pam too had enough. She told her daughter that she was leaving and to call her if she needed a ride.

Peter's cell phone rang; it was his customer from Culver City. The customer needed 50 pills ASAP. He assured his customer that he'll be there in less than an hour. Ignoring Yay-Yay completely, he said to Jazz,

"baby I need you to ride to a customers' with me."

He then kissed her on the cheek and ran into the house to retrieve the product.

Yay-Yay could see that Peter was pissed with her. He rarely made trips to customers' houses; he always sent her or another worker.

He can be mad all he want. He's crazy if he thought I would let him fuck that bitch. If he want to get an attitude so can I.

Yay-Yay then turned to Jazz.

"You stupid."

Jazz had a look of shock on her face.

"How am I stupid?" She asked.

"You didn't say shit. You let that bitch lie in your face about Peter being her homeboy. You know damn well they ain't friends. More like homey, lover, and friends."

Jazz was fed up. Yay- Yay always came at her side ways; especially when it had something to do with Peter. *I swear I think this bitch jealous of me and Peter.*

"Let me tell you something. I'm far from stupid. I may play stupid but I'm not. I know you're a hater and wish you had a man."

"Yay laughed, she then stepped back and looked at her cousin with pity.

"If you only knew boo boo." She said before turning and walking off.

Peter was listening in the doorway. He prayed that Jazz slapped her one good time.

After Yay pulled off, he came out the house and handed Jazz the pills. Her expression read "why I gotta hold them?"

Yay would have taken them with no problem.

"If the police. I said IF, the police pull us over they won't search you. They'll search me because I'm on probation."

She gave him a half-smile.

"K." She said.

****

What you won't do the next one will...

About twenty minutes later Peter was handed a visitors past and he and Jazz pulled into the gated community.

"Get out with me?" He told Jazz. Jazz didn't want to but she did. When they got to the door of the townhouse the door was open. Peter and Jazz walked in. She was a little taken aback by all the white guys that were in the house. The different basketball stuff around the house told her the resident was a fan or a player. A skinny white dude approached Peter. Peter and the dude hugged. He then looked at Jazz but didn't say nothing. Instead he asked Peter,

"Where's the light one with the big ass."

 Jazz was offended. She wanted to snap on his ass, but didn't want to come out of character for a stupid white boy. Besides, he wasn't shit. She'll never see him again. However, she still felt like she should say something.

"Oh, my cousin? She's not working today."

She smiled and held out her hand,

"I'm Jazz; Peter's girlfriend."

Again he ignored her.

"Peter you got that?" He asked.

"Jazz give him the bag." Peter said.

Oh the punk know my name now? Jazz thought as she reached in her purse to retrieve the bag of pills. She then handed them to Pete, but his customer snatched them out of her hand.

"I'm right here." He told her.

That was it. Jazz was about to say something, but someone else spoke up for her.

"Man what the hell is your problem? You don't know how to treat a lady?"

Jazz looked and she didn't know rather to be ashamed or flattered. It was Diesel, Laurie's brother, defending her honor. Diesel put his arm around Jazz neck.

"This is a good friend of the family. Not to mention a great dancer." He smiled looking at her. Jazz was in love with his dimples.

"I think you owe my friend an apology."

"Apology for what, man?" Peter's customer asked.

"Because you don't treat guest..."

"She's not my guest. I invited him not her."

Diesel looked at Peter,

"She is your woman right?"

"Yeah she is." Peter responded while he stared at Diesel's arm around his girl.

"I can't tell." Diesel replied smoothly.

"Anyway. She's a guest, not to mention a good friend. Apologize now. Don't take me there, bruh."

"Diesel it's cool." Jazz said softly.

If she wasn't dancing she hated being in the spotlight. All eyes were on her and she didn't like it.

"No it's not okay." He told her as he admired her silky shoulder length wrap. She had the smoothest dark brown skin he'd ever seen. This girl is gorgeous he thought. Quickly throwing away his thoughts he looked back up at the guy that was buying the product. The guy could see in Diesel's eyes that he was serious. He knew it wasn't a good idea to get on his friend's bad side. He always told D that he had a bad temper.

"I apologize, Jazz." The guy said. He then reached in his pocket, paid Peter and walked over to the couch.

"Sometimes you have to excuse us jocks. We get so caught up in ourselves we forget how to treat others." Diesel told Jazz.

She held her head down.

"It's cool." Jazz said again.

Diesel looked at Peter. He was making him uncomfortable on purpose.

"It's never cool to disrespect a woman. I don't care what her status is. Rich, poor, a ho; it's not cool. Even if she disrespects herself, a man shouldn't help her."

He then put his focus back on Jazz,

"Whenever your around me I'll never let a man disrespect you."

To lighten the mood for Jazz's sake he added,

"I know you can handle the females."

Jazz laughed, "Sure can." She said matter-of-factly.

Is this nigga hitting on my woman in my face? Peter wasn't going to ask what he already knew. "Come on, Jazz." Peter told her.

Diesel gave Jazz one last shot of his dimples and told her he'll see her soon. She said ok and her and Peter walked out the door.

****

Feeling some kind of way........

Peter and Jazz both rode in silence for a good fifteen minutes before he decided to say what was on his mind. He looked over at Jazz. She had her seat leaned back and her eyes closed. Peter knew she wasn't tired and that she was feeling some kind of way about what happened in the house. If she didn't bring it up, neither was he, but he was about to find out who that wanna be black fool was.

"So who was that nigga all on you?" Peter asked.

"He was right there. Why didn't you ask?"

Peter smirked,

"You trying to be funny?"

"Nope."

He took his eyes off the road for a few seconds,

"I asked you a question," He beamed.

Jazz waited a few minutes before she replied. She was debating if she should get smart, being that she was mad that he didn't defend her in the house, or just tell him who Prince Charming was. *OMG* Jazz thought; *did I just call Diesel Prince Charming?*

"That's Diesel. Laurie's brother."

Peter didn't respond. He thought about Diesel's status, which was one of the star players at USC, and then he thought about Jazz's status: an above average girl from the ghetto who was Diesel's sister's friend. He wrote Diesel's actions off as being nice.

"Why did you let that guy disrespect me?"

I knew that was coming Peter thought.

To be honest, he would fight tigers and bears for Jazz he truly cared about the girl.

The only reason why he allowed the guy to be so rude was to see if Jazz would check his ass. If that was Yay-Yay it wouldn't have went down like that. Yay wasn't the type you would want to make your girl; she was just cool to be around. He knew Yay was just using him for his paper and his good sex game. He also knew that Yay was a shady bitch and if she even suspected that he would cut her off from the money and dick without her approval, Peter would have hell to pay. Apart from all that she could hold her own. Jazz only did when she was forced. He didn't like that. Sometimes he wished he could take some of Yay qualities(light skin, big butt and confidence) and mixed them with everything he loved about Jazz and then he would have the perfect girl.

"Peter you heard me." Jazz snapped, breaking Peter's thoughts.

"Heard what?" He said.

"Why in the hell did you let him talk to me like that?"

Peter pulled in front of Jazz's house and cut off the car. He looked at her, "he was just playing. Stop getting mad over small stuff." Then he had the nerve to try and kiss her. Jazz moved her head back, opened the car door, got out, slammed it and went into the

****

She got that good good...

Peter pulled up in front of his house, parked his car and got out. He shook his head when he saw Yay-Yay parked blocking his drive way.

"I don't know why you shaking your head." Yay said as she waited for Peter to unlock his gate.

"What you doing over here? I don't appreciate that shit you pulled today."

"And I don't appreciate you trying to talk to that ho in my face."

"You ain't my girl. I don't say nothing about them niggas you mess with. You know why? Because I'm not your man.

you got feelings?"

Peter opened the front door, he allowed Yay to walk in first and then he went in after her.

"Nigga, If I wanted to be your girl I can. You and I both know that."

"Yeah; alright." Peter said as he walked over to the bar and made him a drink.

"You still haven't told me what you doing over here?"

"Waiting on you."

He took a swallow from his glass.

"Waiting on me? How you know when, or if I was coming home?"

She flopped down on the couch, and took off her shoes.

"I knew you were coming back. You only went to drop that bitch off. I saw y'all on the I105"

He looked at her,

"What you stalking me? And that's your peoples, why she gotta be a bitch?"

"Nigga stalk you? Don't flatter yourself. I came for two reasons; I need some dick and some money. And you have both."

She stood up and took off her pants, then her shirt. Peter got hard staring at her in her pink lace bra and panty set. *After today I ain't fucking with her no more.* Peter tried to convince himself.

"Oh and she's a bitch because I said so. That's my cousin; I can call her what I want."

Peter walked over to her, "shut up" he said and then pushed her on the couch. The two made passionate sex all night.

If don't make dollars it don't make sense….

Chapter 4

When Savanna told her guy about the business proposal Diesel offered, and how she did not have any girls in mind to do the party with her, he came up with an plan of his own. He and Savanna would go to the club on her off day to pick the girls and approach them with the proposition himself. No way was he going to allow them to miss out on some real paper because she was too selfish to ask any of the girls for help. Although he'd been to the club over a hundred times watching the same girls shake they asses, and in his mind he knew who would be a good candidate to get the job done, he decided to get Savanna involved, give her some say as to who she could bare to work with and who was flat out of the question. So on her day off from the club, the two of them went together on a stripper scout.

A young dark skin girl with an oversized booty had just finished her show. White-Girl went to ask her guy what he thought of her and got sidetracked. She turned up her nose as she watched her co-worker walk in like she was all that and a bag of chips.

Yay-Yay, better known as Delicious when stepping into the Starz Gentlemen Club, is one confident black bitch and White-Girl couldn't stand her. It wasn't a secret that the bitch was shady. No shady is an understatement; the bitch is straight cut throat. From what White-Girl witnessed she's the type that wants what she wants and won't stop at nothing to get it. So you know the winch didn't have a problem with stealing her co-workers clients from right in front of them. She seen her do it numerous of times. That was not what she had against her. Business is business, there is always somebody better then you, somebody trying to compete against you and somebody that can and will steal what you have in a blink of an eye. That's why you had to be on point at all times, alert, and aware of the competition so when they strike you can stop them. Even if you can't stop them you gotta give them one hell of a fight otherwise you're fucked. They are going to take it all. When White-Girl came to the club three months ago she came already trained and with her mind on green. She was schooled years ago by her home girl, Mercedes, on how to get it. Mercedes taught her that green talks and bullshit walks. She told her that when doing anything, do it with a purpose. She worked the club and fucked with a few dudes after hours to help stack enough money to move out on her own comfortably. She had only been out of jail for about a year; she had a little money saved, but not enough to say that she was on her feet. Her guy could think all he wanted that he had a bimbo on his team. She's nowhere near it. She might look like Pamela Anderson but she is far from a dumb blonde. Just like he had her on his team for a purpose, she played for his team for a purpose. Both of their motives are to use the other to make money. White-Girl could have tried to make money on her own, but she felt in a new city: "Home of The Angels", she needed protection; especially doing what she did. She met ol' boy a few months after she got out of jail. She was working as a waitress over at Roscoe's. She was attracted to him the first day he tried to holler. She always had a thing for black guys and he's attractive so that was a bonus. He got extra points because of his swag; a bad boy with charm. He kind of reminded her of a guy she once loved, a guy that by accident rescued her from the fucked up hand of life she was dealt. Within a year of being with him, his grimy, powder head ass was starting to disgust her and she couldn't wait until she came up with a master plan and or stacked enough paper to get away from him.

In the meantime, he was her "Daddy" and she was not about to allow a sassy, grimy, envious ghetto girl take him from her. That was the main reason why she couldn't stand Delicious. The bitch was disrespectful. It did not take a rocket scientist to know that the dude that picked her up and dropped her off at the club was more than a client. That bitch, Delicious, knew that, she just didn't give a damn and thought that White-Girl would sit quietly and watch her flirt with her dude, whenever she thought he was looking. She was fooled. She learned that when the waitress walked over, handed her dude a glass of cognac and then pointed over at Delicious to let him know who sent it. White-Girl got up from her seat. She slowly walked over to where Delicious was sitting with her friend Paris. She spoke to Paris and Paris spoke back. Delicious acted like she didn't see her walk over to the table. White -Girl walked over to her, leaned down and whispered in her ear,

"That drink you sent over to my man, you're going to need that to calm your nerves when I'm done."

Delicious moved her head away from White-Girl and gave her a look that said, bitch please. White-Girl smiled and whispered the words, "I can show you better than I can tell you."

White-Girl walked over to the DJ booth. She smiled at him. He smiled back and threw his head up. The two was cool, he was the reason the owner gave her a chance to try out and prove that "Whatever a black girl can do she can do it too, if not better." The DJ stepped out the booth and walked down to see what she wanted. She had to want something. She was standing there. When the DJ approached her she motioned him to lean forward so she could whisper in his ear the nature of her visit. She then held up a hundred dollar bill. He looked at her debating if he wanted to risk being chewed out by the other girls or go home with some extra cash. "Money talks, bullshit walks" is what White-Girl thought when he took the bill from her hand. She then sashayed back over toward her table. She made sure she added some spunk to her runway model walk when she passed by Delicious. She grabbed her bag and whispered in her guy's ear. He gave her a nod and she headed for the dressing room. She walked to her locker, pulled out her key and opened up the locker. "If you stay ready, you ain't gotta get ready." She thought and she undressed down to her black thong with the matching bustier. After she put her street clothes into her locker, she grabbed her smell goods and put some on. She then touched up her make-up and waited for the DJ to play her song.

Inside the club the lights went dim and the beat from Ciara's song Ride It surfaced throughout the building

"I'm going to fuck him up." Yay said when she heard her song. She added, "I know none of these amateurs ain't trying to work my song."

"Okayy..." Paris said.

The DJ announced,

"White-Girl is about to show us how she ride. Y'all niggas ready for this?"

Paris and Delicious looked at each other and then at the stage. White-Girl walked out with a red Trench coat on and a pair of stilettos. She was lip singing the lyrics to the song as she dropped her coat to the floor:

"I can do it big I can do it long...I can do it whenever or however you want..."

She twirled her hips round and round in slow motion. She switched the rotation and wiggled like a snake all the way to the floor... She dropped to her knees and positioned herself like she was sitting on a hard Pogo Stick.

"I can do it up and down I can do it in circles...." She sang as she moved her body matching the lyrics.

That bitch doing it Paris thought to herself.

White-Girl looked at Delicious and nodded her head up and down like, yeah bitch."

Making sure she bounced her ass extra hard she quickly got up off the ground. Still staring at Delicious she rotated her body, pointed at herself and sang ,

"I market it so gooood..... they can't wait to... try... I I I... Meh... Aaaa...I work it so gooood.... Man, these niggas tryna buy... I I I I... me.....He like the way I ride it...!!!"

Dat part right there was the truth. White-girl already had a large fan base but the shit she was doing had them niggas head's spinning. They were throwing money. A few girls that worked there were even cheering for her; some threw her money just to fuck with Delicious. They was happy somebody out did that bitch. White-Girl continued to work the song. Close to the end, she made her way over to her guy, again she looked at Delicious. This time Delicious ignored her. White-Girl still did her thang..."

He like the way I ride it...He like the way I ride it..." She sang while giving her guy a lap dance.

The song ended and the crowed gave her a round of applause. On her way back to the stage to collect her winnings she walked back pass Delicious, bent over close enough so she could hear her,

"whatever you can do there is a white bitch that can do it better." She said, snapped her fingers twice and walked off.

Love all over me......

Chapter 5

Jazz walked in the house high on love. She enjoyed a wonderful day with Peter at Santa Monica Pier. Peter won her teddy bears, they rode the Ferris wheel, took pictures, and walked on the beach holding hands. Jazz listened while Peter apologized for the way he'd been acting. He also told her that he thought about it and he should have checked the dude in Culver City for coming at her like she was a rat. She told him it was okay, but he better speak up if anything like that happened again. They kissed. She could feel Peter's friend rise in his pants. She smiled and told him one more month. Peter sighed and stepped back. He looked at her and told her that she was beautiful and how he admired her for keeping her goodies off limits until she was ready. He also told her that he appreciated, and felt honored that she was going to allow him to take away her pureness. Chills ran through Jazz when she thought about it. She enjoyed the oral sex, but she couldn't wait until her baby blew her back out as Yay-Yay would say. Thinking about Yay-Yay, Jazz thought she may as well tell Peter how she felt.

"Peter I know you consider Yay-Yay as family." - She noticed his eye brow rise. - She continued, "but I think the girl has a crush on you." She paused and waited for Peter's response. To her surprise he didn't defend Yay-Yay like he did in the past. He must feel the same way Jazz thought. She took a deep breath.

"Peter. I don't want my cousin working for you."

"What?" Peter blurted. He wasn't expecting to hear that one. Unsure of how to respond to Jazz' request, Peter charmed her. He pulled her close to him, kissed her soft lips and said,

"Let's not mess up tonight talking about Yay-Yay or any other female; it's me and your time."

She smiled and nodded to agree.

"Can we talk about it later, she asked Pete.

He told her yes, later, but not now. Then they kissed again.

Later that night they ended back up at his place. Once the two got their buzz on, Peter started by pleasuring Jazz and to his surprise it ended with her pleasuring him. Although she wasn't experienced with performing oral sex like Yay was, Peter focused on who was doing it and how much he loved and appreciated her. He wasn't able to bust, but that was okay. He still enjoyed every minute of her attempt to please him. Around 2am Peter dropped Jazz off at home.

Before day break on Friday morning.........

Peter pulled his silver 745 in front of the black iron gate that lead to the entrance of his driveway. He put his car in park, got out and unlocked his gate. He walked back to his car, got in, shut the door and pulled into his driveway. He cut his car off and sat there for a minute. A smile crept across his face when he thought about Jazz and how she tried to please him. He puffed his chest out thinking about how he had a young tender that was still a virgin, smart, pretty and loved him like no other. She's definitely someone he would want to wife in the future. She was one of the only ones that accepted him for him. And he loved her for that. The only problem he had was having his ego stroked. That's why he fucked around with the hood rats and gold diggers they catered to his ego. They made him feel like he was the man, a king. They were impressed with his status. Jazz cared nothing about that. All she cared about was that he was her man. Status, money, cars was never the reason she chose to be in love with Peter. And he knew that. *I promise I'm going to do right by her as soon as she let me break her in.* Peter thought. The sounds of E40's Tell Me When to Go broke Peter out of his thoughts. He looked in his rearview mirror and noticed Sabrina getting out of a black Yukon. *A different nigga every other night,* Peter thought to his self as he got out the car and walked toward the gate to lock it.

"What's up, Peter?" Sabrina said as she crossed the street.

"Come here, Sabrina." He called out.

With no questions asked, she sashayed over to Peter. He checked her out. She was slutty-looking good. She wore a white halter mini dress and a pair of red stilettos, to match her fire engine red hair. Just looking at her, Peter got hard. It was something about them light skin ghetto girls that turned him on.

"Ain't it too late for you to be out?" Peter teased.

"I'm grown." Sabrina shot back. "Anyway, what's up?" she asked.

"You wanna smoke something?"

"I don't smoke." She frowned her lips and looked him up and down real quick. "But if you got something to drink I'm with that. I'm going to need a buzz to block out my granny bitching."

She looked over at her house.

"I know she ain't sleep."

Peter unlocked his front gate.

"Come on."

Sabrina took two steps into the yard and before Peter could shut the gate good, the driver of the Yukon swooped up in front of his house. A brown skin dude, with cornrows jumped out with a pistol in his hand. His eyes were on Sabrina and his gun was pointed at Peter. The nigga was smooth. That's because he was a gangster first and a pimp second.

"Bitch, you think this a game?"

Sabrina held her hands in a surrender position and shook her head no. She was more in shock then scared. He then looked at Peter.

"What you had planned with my bitch?"

Peter's punk ass was scared as shit and it was written in his voice and on his face. He never did no fighting or shooting. He really didn't have problems. He was a cool cat. Any problems he had Ken would handle them for him. Peter swallowed hard. He stared at the barrel of the gun. Slowly he answered,

"Nothing. We was going to have a drink. It ain't even like that."

Old boy then looked back at Sabrina.

"How much you charge him?"

"We... We... Charge him, for what?"

He walked over to Sabrina and *Bow:* Slapped the shit out of her causing her to fall on her ass. He then kicked her in her right leg.

"You think this shit a game?" He scolded her.

"Daddy, I'm sorry." She said.

He looked at her and frowned.

"Get up bitch."

She held her face and continued to sit there on the ground. She was in shock; she was scared to move. When she didn't do as he said, he picked her up by her hair. She let out a light scream.

"Don't make me fuck you up. Shut your mouth and go get in the truck."

She wanted to tell him she had to go in the house. She'd been gone for two days. The only reason why her granny hadn't filled out a missing persons report is because she had been calling her, telling her she was alright. Sabrina felt in her gut that her fast ways had caught up with her. Her granny was right. She done got herself in some shit she couldn't get out of. Sabrina did as she was told and walked to the truck and got in it.

I gotta get away from this nigga, but I'm scared. How about he kills me like he said?

She thought about the night she told him that she wanted to be his, and when he agreed to claim her, he warned her that if she ever gave his pussy away she better get some money for it. He also told her if she ever tried to leave he would kill her. He only let her check in with her granny to keep the police off his back.

Peter didn't know what to think. He didn't know if he should have remorse for Sabrina or be scared for his life.

I should have taken my ass in the house. Ken said my dick was going to be the death of me. Shit I pictured dying in some pussy because it was just that good, but not getting killed over it.

"I'm sorry homey." Peter said.

Old boy gave Peter a once over. His gear was on point. He then looked in the yard at the 745 and Cadillac truck. Either he had money or he was flossing. Whatever it was, he was going to break bread or get fucked up.

He looked at Peter.

"You see that's my bitch. My property. Looking is alright. I see you looking when I dropped her off, and I was cool with that. It's when you trespass that causes a problem."

"I never...!"

The pimp put his hand to his lips to hush Peter.

"Don't talk unless you are asked."

He looked over at his truck. Sabrina's lip was fucked up.

"Fucking with you, she's going to be off for two days. You owe me. Point, blank, period. I need three hundred dollars." he told Peter.

Without hesitation Peter reached in his pocket and pulled out about seven hundred dollars. He went to count out three hundred, but was told to hand it all over. He was going to protest until he saw the look in the pimp/robber/gangster's face.

"Here, man." Pete said. "Can a nigga get some head for the extra I threw in?" Pete joked nervously.

The pimp smiled.

"As a matter of fact you can." He only agreed for three reasons. One, to prove a point by letting Sabrina know he meant what he said. She belonged to him. Two, to gain a customer. He could tell Pete was weak for pussy. Three, to get inside of Pete's house to see what he was all about. Maybe Peter will be his next lick. He looked at the truck;

"Sexy come to daddy."

Is this nigga crazy? He just fucked me up. Now I'm sexy. Come to daddy?

Sabrina got out and walked over to the daddy she never had. He grabbed her by the hair.

"Bitch, you ain't no tramp. Go put your shoes on."

She did. When she returned the pimp looked at Peter.

"Let's go inside."

I was just playing, is what Peter wanted to say, but his dick and heart was saying something different.

The three walked in the house.

"Your shit is the business." The Pimp said admiring Peter's expensive furniture and the topnotch liquor that sat on his wet bar. He was really digging the 62 inch plasma T.V.

"Thanks, man. Shit I spent enough on this shit." Peter bragged.

He looked over at Sabrina. Her lip was busted. She looked helpless. Peter felt bad for her.

"Aye. Can I give her a towel or something for her face?"

"Yeah. That's cool."

Peter walked off to the back and came back with a face towel. He handed it to the pimp and told him he was welcome to the bathroom. The pimp whispered in Sabrina's ear to put on her big girl panties. He told her if she tried anything stupid or embarrassed him, she would regret it.

"Now smile." He said and she did.

When she got up to go to the restroom, Peter offered him a drink. He had a choice of XO Hennessy or Patron. Old boy chose XO for him and Patron for Sabrina. Peter, feeling guilty about what he was about to let Sabrina do to him, thought he would help her out by crumbling an X pill in her drink.

"By the way I'm Peter." He said out the blue as he handed the pimp both drinks.

"Wack."

"Wack?" Peter laughed. "A pimp called Wack?"

"The bitches call me daddy." He was stern.

Peter's phone beeped indicating his battery was dead. Thanks to Yay-Yay. She had been texting and calling him all night.

"Bitch don't get the hint." Peter spoke out loud on purpose.

"You smoke?" Wack asked, ignoring his comment.

"Hell yeah. I smoke that good shit."

Peter went behind his wet bar and pulled out a box. He then handed it to Wack. Wack opened the box and smiled. It was filled with Kush.

"Nigga, I'm going to have to take some of this home."

He laughed. But Wack was for real.

"It's cool. I got the hook up. Take some. Ziploc bags right there." He pointed to the glass table in the den.

Sabrina finally came back out the restroom. She looked a little more fresh. But her lip was still messed up.

I hope she can suck it. Peter thought.

"Here", Wack said handing Sexy her drink.

She took it and sat it down on the table.

"Down it." Wack ordered.

Her hands were shaking as she put the drink to her mouth and drank every drop. Peter hurried up and walked over and took the cup from Sabrina. He was scared residue would be left in the glass.

Boom....Boom....Boom.....

Peter looked at Wack. Wack looked at Sabrina. Peter looked at the door. Sabrina prayed it was God answering her prayer by sending someone to save her.

Boom...Boom...Boom....

"Peter I know you in there. Open the door."

It was Yay-Yay.

"Damn." Peter mumbled. He forgot to lock the gate.

"That's your bitch?" Wack asked.

*Thanks for nothing God...*Sabrina thought.

Peter knew Yay wouldn't leave unless she got what she came for. Peter looked at Wack.

"Hold up." He said and walked by the door.

"What man? What you want?" He questioned.

"Nigga, what you mean what? Open the door." She ordered.

"For what? I'm busy."

"Busy? Busy? You better not have no bitch up in here."

"And if I did so what. You ain't my bitch."

"Nigga who you fronting for? You don't even be acting hard like that. Anyway, I need some work bitches from the club been sweating me and I ain't got shit. Why you all up on pussy you missing money. Now open the damn door."

"Man let her in. She too loud." Wack said.

 Peter obeyed.

Yay walked in the house with a nasty frown on her face. She rolled her eyes at Peter. She then looked at Sabrina. She shook her head. She was about to make a comment about her busted lip, but when she noticed the dude that was sitting next to Sabrina, he caught her by surprise. It was the dude from the club; the one that she wanted, but couldn't stand because he messed with White-Girl. Wack smirked at Yay-Yay's uneasiness. Yay rolled her eyes.

"How you know him?" She asked walking over to the bar to make herself a drink.

"He the homey; why?"

"Homey. Humph."

 She looked at Sabrina.

"Don't tell me his white bitch bust your lip?"

She shook her head as if it was true. Wack smiled. He knew Yay was taking a shot at him. He also knew that she had a little crush on him and was mad because she wasn't use to being ignored. What she did not know was that he was digging her too, but his focus at the time was getting his hoes trained to trust him and obey. So far, he only had Sabrina and Savannah, which neither knew about the other. But it would not be long before he had his stable in order. He didn't have time for Yay-Yay' ass. A girl of her caliber was trouble: A straight drama queen.

Sabrina could not respond to Yay's question if she wanted to. The effects from the pill and the alcohol were taking control over her. She sat there quietly trying to understand what the voices in her head were telling her. Yay didn't know that Sabrina was under the influence. All she knew was that she was getting ignored. And she did not like it.

"What you can't talk?" She asked Sabrina. She then looked at Wack, "Can you tell her to answer my question?"

"Little momma you don't know me. Keep your mouth shut." Wack said.

Wack's gaze told Yay that he wasn't like the other dudes she got smart with. He was to be taken seriously. But it was too late to back down now.

"You don't know yourself. You're confused." Yay shot back.

"Why you coming at that man like that?" Peter intervened.

"Shut up." She told Peter.

"I ain't tripping off that immature shit."

Immature, she thought? She'd never been called that before. A bitch, stuck-up, sassy, and a whole bunch of other names that described her character well, but immature? She was a little embarrassed by the comment. Instead of getting smart she spoke to Peter.

"Peter I need 100 of them." Yay said.

Peter looked at Wack,

"I'll be back. Let me handle this. Y'all can make yourself another drink if you want to. Fire up something."

He walked down the hall into his guest room/office to retrieve the product. In his mind he promised his self that he wasn't going to fuck with Yay anymore in no kind of way; she was starting to be too much trouble. Every day it got worst.

Wack got up and made him another drink. Yay watched Sabrina as she stared in space. She wanted to ask Sabrina what her young ass was doing over there, but went against it. Wack eyed Yay as he stood at the bar pouring his drink. Yay glanced over at him, but turned her head. It was something about him that mad her uncomfortable. To hide her nervousness, she picked up the Ink magazine off the coffee table. She began to flip through the pages. She could feel Wack still staring at her. She couldn't hold her tongue any longer.

"What, damn!" She said, looking up from the magazine.

Wack did not respond. She looked up at him.

"Something got your tongue?" She smirked like she was amused.

"That shit ain't attractive." He told her.

"Neither is the white bitch you fucking." She said, and jumped up from the stool she was sitting on, and walked over to Peter who was making his way back into the living room. Peter handed her the bag of pills.

"I gave you 150 just in case." He told her.

"Do I call you or Ken?" She asked.

"Ken." He said.

"That's fine." She put her hands on her hips and added, "I need three hundred dollars."

"Take it out of that."

Peter was referring to the money she would make off the pills.

"Whatever."

Yay walked back over to the bar, poured a little Patron in a glass, and in one gulp she drank it. She then grabbed her purse and headed for the door. Yay paused in her tracks and turned to confirm what she was hearing. Sabrina was vomiting all over the place. Wack and Peter looked at the girl like they were disgusted. It was their fault she was fucked up. The three of them watched her puke for a good sixty seconds. When she was done she began to cry. This stupid ass girl trying to be grown, now look at her. Yay thought. "What the fuck did y'all give this girl?" Yay scolded when Sabrina started taking off her dress. She was sweating and then she started throwing up again.

"She only had a glass of vodka", Peter said nervously.

Yay looked at him. *That nigga probably slipped her something.*

"Peter, get her ass some milk now." Yay yelled. "Help me get her to the bathroom." She told Wack.

She knew what to do. Her mother is a pill head. There has been plenty of times her mother took too much and Yay had to nurse her back to health; she hated her mother and often wished she died, but she nursed her back to health whenever she had too much. Wack assisted Yay with getting Sabrina to the bathroom. Once they were in there, Yay turned the shower on cold. Peter came back with the milk. Yay took it from his hand. She put it up to Sabrina's mouth.

"Here baby drink this. It's going to make you feel better." She told Yay.

Sabrina took a couple of big sips before she knocked the glass out of Yay's hand.

"No, I don't want anymore. You guys are trying to kill me." She cried, "I just want my mommy."

"No, we're trying to help you feel better. Come on get in the shower. It's going to help sober you up."

"Come on. Help me get this girl in the shower y'all."

Wack and Peter did as Yay asked.

"Ahhh… it's cold," Sabrina screamed when the water touched her. She laid her head against the shower wall and cried to herself... "Mommy, why did you leave me? You should have taken me with you. Now look what happened." Sabrina continued to cry. Sabrina never knew her parents, but she did know of her mother. Her foster granny told her that her mother, Stacy White, left her with her when she was five months old. She said that she was going back to California to attend her grandfather's funeral. She didn't want to take Sabrina because the bus trip from Louisiana to Cali was three days. They both agreed that was too long for a little baby. Well that trip turned into fourteen and a half years. When Sabrina turned twelve, she and her foster granny moved back down to California. She thought it would be a great idea since she had a business there and an even better opportunity for Sabrina. Sabrina wanted to be a model. Everyone knows Hollywood is the best place to be discovered. Unfortunately, the grimy streets of Los

Scandalous, also known as Los Angeles, got a hold of Sabrina before Hollywood did.

Yay stared at the needy little girl as she poured her heart out on the shower floor. She knew the feeling of wanting to be loved. Unlike Sabrina, she grew up in the house with her mother, still lives with her, but there was no mother-daughter love between the two. It was safe to say that Yay and her mother hated each other. Looking at Sabrina shed tears over someone that obviously wasn't thinking about or cared about her, kind of pissed her off. Yay thought that Sabrina needed a backbone. Why cry over something you did not have the power to change? That's how Yay felt about it. She was not going to force anyone to give a fuck about her. "It's me against the word!" was her attitude. She'll learn that one day. I hope sooner than later. Yay thought.

"I got her. Y'all can go back in there and do what y'all do." Yay told Wack and Peter.

Yay did not have to tell them twice. Without hesitation, the two left Sabrina and Yay in the bathroom.

Minutes later, Sabrina stopped crying and tried to get up off the floor. Yay leaned in the shower and cut the water off. She then reached over and tried to help Sabrina up.

"You okay?" Yay was sincere.

Sabrina shook her head no.

"My head hurts." She cried.

"Once you go to sleep and wake back up, you'll be alright. Come on, let's get out these clothes." She told her.

Yay helped Sabrina undress and handed her a towel to wrap her body in; she then escorted her to Peter's room where she gave her a pair of Peter's sweats and a T-shirt to put on.

"I'm taking her home." She told Wack and Peter, upon entering the living room.

"Why?" Wack asked. She hadn't made good on her deal. Peter did pay for a piece of her.

"Because she's sick and she wanna go home. If she's interested in you when she sobers up, she'll call you." Yay snapped. He was beginning to turn her off.

"I'll call you tomorrow I promise." Sabrina told Wack.

"You owe this man." Wack said pointing at Peter.

"No. No. She don't owe me anything. I'm good." Peter said.

He felt Yay staring him. He hoped that she did not figure out what was going on.

Wack stared at Sabrina. She looked so much prettier without all the make-up. She looked so innocent, so pure, and so familiar. Was it her hazel colored eyes that reminded him of his older brother Bent? Or was it her hair? The shower made it curly. She kind of looked like his mother and his baby sister Keysha. Maybe it was guilt. Maybe he was feeling bad that he was going to be part of the reason her life falls apart. It was something, but at that moment he wasn't about to try and figure it out. He needed to allow Yay's nosy ass to take her home; the girl did need to check-in with her grandmother. When he was ready for her, he knew where to find her.

Wack nodded his head to agree with Sabrina leaving.

Yay walked over and picked up her purse from the table. She then walked back over to Sabrina and took her by the hand. She looked at Wack,

"That's how you do us sisters, huh?"

Wack felt like he did not have to respond to her comment. And he didn't.

Yay looked at Peter.

"You wouldn't want nobody to do Jazz like that."

She shook her head as she and Sabrina walked out the door. Peter went behind them to shut the door and lock it.

That was crazy.... Wack pulled him away from his thought.

  "Man before you do some shit again let me know what's going on. You can't be just lacing somebody shit like that." Wack told Peter.

"I apologize about that. I was just trying to loosen her up."

"I hear you. Aye I'm about to bounce. But give me your number so I can get at you. I see you got those thangs on lock."

He was talking about the X he saw him give Yay-Yay.

"My nigga got some good ass whole sale prices. I probably can get you a deal."

Wack handed Peter his phone and told him to put his number in. Peter took the phone from Wack's hand and put his number in. When he was done, he handed the phone back to Wack.

.

"I'm the supplier. Me and my people make it ourselves."

"You bullshitting?" Wack asked. He was surprised.

That nigga making paper. Thought Wack.

"Nope. We been on for a few years now. Niggas used to say we were some nerds, because Ken and me stayed in the lab or my garage experimenting. People did not know what we were doing. We was trying to come up with a pill to cure breast cancer. At the time my mom's had it. Ken's grandmother had already died from it. When my mom's died, we did not see the purpose no more, so we left it alone. We stopped messing in the lab altogether. We kicked back for a few months. Then Ken came up with an idea to make some money. Everybody was off that X, so he was like fuck it, let's make that. It took some time. It was well worth it because we on now. Ken's about to go to New Orleans, help his moms get settled in, and while he's out there he's going to try to expand our shit out there. We trying to put that West Coast Fire on the map."

West Coast Fire, Wack thought. He heard about it; niggas said the shit was the business. It's the red pill with the WC on the front and the flames on the back.

Wack smiled at his luck.

 "I might can help you expand. We going to talk, little homey."

"Thanks man. Get at me. Aye, call my phone so I can have your number." Peter said.

"Alright." Wack said and walked out.

Drama, don't you sleep?

Chapter 6

Jazz looked at her clock; it was almost 5am. What the hell did Yay-Yay want?

"Hello." Jazz answered in her gurgle voice.

"Um. My bad for waking you. But I thought you may wanna know what your man did."

No, she is not calling me about Peter. What the hell is up with that? Jazz thought.

"I haven't talked to you in three days. And when I do it's about Peter. Isn't Peter the reason you stopped talking to me?"

"Look I ain't got time for all that extra shit. Whining and stuff. Grow up. Do you wanna know what I gotta say or not?"

"Not!" Jazz said and ended the call.

Yay looked at her phone. No this bitch didn't. She dialed Jazz's number back. Jazz hit ignored and then cut her phone off.

I wonder if Peter cut her ass off like I suggested. I'll ask tomorrow.

The Next Day

Jazz stood in front of the studio waiting for Peter to pick her up. The two were going to see a movie then have dinner. Jazz turned to the sound of Laurie's voice.

"You want me to wait with you?"

"No I'm good." Jazz said.

Laurie looked across the parking lot.

"Girl, look; she all on my brother." Laurie said, referring to one of the dance instructors.

Jazz shook her head.

"What, girl? Why you shaking your head?"

Diesel saw that too. He wondered why she shook her head and hoped Laurie would tell him.

"Because he just had that white girl in the car, now her? Guys are a trip."

"He a ho. What you expect; he a ball player."

"I know right."

Both Laurie and Jazz laughed.

"Let me go pee real quick." Laurie told Jazz.

Laurie then turned to go back in the building.

"You going to get enough about peeing in public restrooms. Something going to jump out on you."

"I rather that, then pissing on myself."

Laurie walked back in the building to use the restroom.

Jazz glanced back over at Diesel. *She all on him. I could have sworn she said she had a man. I guess they made for each other. Like Laurie* said, *he ain't nothing but a ho.* Diesel looked up and caught Jazz's stare. She turned her head. *Peter needs to hurry up.* She then thought about Yay's call last night. *I wonder what happened between the two.* Jazz went in her bag and pulled out her cell phone and dialed her voicemail. The first message put a smile on her face. It was Peter... *Baby I love you. I can't wait to see you today.* Message number two, erased her smile. *It was Yay-Yay. I know your immature ass didn't hang up on me. It ain't my fault your nigga foul. I was just trying to let your silly ass know that Peter has no respect for you. You so stupid."* Jazz shook her head. Message three was Yay-Yay again. *"You know what. I'm going to tell you because you're my cousin. Peter is a ho. He's scandalous. He had Sabrina's young ass over there about 3:30 this morning. If I hadn't come over to pick up the work, no telling what would have happened. The little girl was not only drunk, but he laced her drink. I saved her by taking her home. I saved Peter's perverted ass too. If her grandmother would have found out his ass would be in jail. That's some desperate ass shit."* Jazz was heated. If Peter was in front of her she would have knocked his head off. How dare he? She thought.

Laurie walked up. She noticed her friend's mood.

"You okay?"

"I'm good. Just wait right here. I may be leaving with you."

Laurie was about to ask her what happened, but Peter pulled up and Jazz walked to his car. She opened the door and sat inside. She left the car door open on purpose.

"I thought I asked you not to allow my cousin to work for you anymore."

"Damn. That's how you get at me? While she telling you I gave her work, she didn't tell you that Ken fired her ass. She claims her momma stole her work. That's what she mad about. Her momma ain't took that shit, she just trying to get over."

If she said that then most likely it's true. That sound like auntie. Jazz thought.

Peter added,

"If she wasn't family, Ken would have gotten something done to her."

"Nobody ain't going to do shit to my cousin."

"I know 'cuz that's your peeps. Now shut the door so we can go."

"Was Sabrina at your house? Did you lace her drink?"

Peter scrunched up his forehead and tiny beads of sweat formed on the top of his nose. Peter only does that for two reasons. He's either nervous or lying, or both.

"There you go. Always coming at me with what somebody said."

"That's a lie and you know it. Now answer my question!"

"It wasn't even like that."

"I can't believe you." Jazz cried," You was going to fuck her? Damn Peter." She got out the car.

Peter jumped out too. He ran toward her.

"Come here, Jazz. It wasn't like that. That was the homey boy girl"

"The homey? Tell me why in the hell would you lace your homey's girl's drink?"

"Can you just get in the car. I'll tell you in the car."

The security walked over and asked was everything ok. Peter told him yeah.

"No, it's not. This man won't leave me alone."

"Sir, if you don't leave I'm going to call the police."

Peter looked at Jazz ; he then glanced at Laurie and her brother who were watching.

"You not going to leave with me?" He asked.

She ignored him and walked off , heading toward the parking lot where Diesel and Laurie waited.

Chapter 7

Jazz and Laurie sat in the dining room talking about their past and future. It wasn't that Diesel was trying to eavesdrop on Jazz and Laurie conversation, it was just that Laurie had a high pitch, squeaky voice that echoed throughout the mansion. It didn't make it any better that they were in the family room and he was in the den right next to them. When the girls were through talking, he learned that Jazz was still a virgin. That sort of shocked him since most girls her age was already given it up; including his sister. Not to mention the high percentage of teen pregnancy. But not Jazz, that diva refused to put out until she was eighteen.

"No babies until I finish college and my husband and I purchase our first home. I refuse to be a welfare recipient mom, living in a low-income,   Mexican neighborhood or the projects." Jazz stated.

"I feel you girl." Laurie replied.

The girls sat in their own thoughts for a minute.

 "So are you really done with Peter?"

Before Jazz could respond, Laurie added,

"How you know Yay's messy ass ain't exaggerating. You know your cousin's messy."

"Yay is messy, but the thing is, she be telling the truth. And plus I know when Peter is lying. I mean damn, I'm not stupid. I know the nigga was sleeping with other females. I didn't care as long as they weren't anybody I knew. And it wasn't in my face. He only had a little over a month, and I was his. He couldn't even wait. He trying to practically rape a 15 year old whore."

Jazz frowned her face thinking about how low Pete was willing to go just for some ass.

"I mean damn. People already think he a nasty ho. Yay couldn't wait to throw that shit in my face."

Tears began to fall.

"I really love that boy. I trusted him. I accepted him for him. Not for what he got. Niggas don't appreciate a real one when they got it. Ughh... I hate that Yay caught him. "

"Girl, forget her. Why you always worried about what she think? She can't judge nobody. She a ho."

Jazz chuckled,

"she's a stripper not a ho."

"Whatever. But let me go put this food up and clean the kitchen before my momma come down and have a fit. You staying the night or do you want my brother to take you home?"

"I'mma stay."

"Good, we'll finish this convo when I'm done." Laurie got up and headed for the kitchen.

Jazz got up, straightened the couch pillows back, cut the radio off and headed toward Laurie's room. She bumped into Diesel coming around the corner.

"Hey", she said and smiled.

"Hey, yourself." He smiled back exposing his deep dimples.

The lights from the chandelier caused his blue eyes to sparkle. They stared at each other for about a minute before Jazz tried to walk off.

"Where are you going?" He said, grabbing her hand.

He looked into her eyes. It's true that you can read the depth of a person's soul just by looking into their eyes. Her eyes say, she can be trusted and she wanted to trust. Her eyes said that her love is 100. Her eyes say that she yearned for Mr. Right to give her love. Her eyes said, that she was attracted to Diesel just as he was attracted to her. And that pleased him. However, her eyes said, I'm scared that you may hurt me. And I wouldn't give you that chance. Jazz looked down at Diesel's big hands on her tiny wrist. She then looked back up at him. She spoke softly, "is there something you wanna talk about?

"I was wondering if you would like to go to the Lakers game next week?"

Why would I ask a girl to the Lakers game? Damn, D, you couldn't think of nothing else?

Jazz's smile was big as the Pacific Ocean and bright as a sunny day in Cali.

"Heck, yes I wanna go. Laurie know I love some Fisher."

He smiled again.

"Oh, yeah?"

"Yeah; she didn't tell you? Of course not; she don't care about basketball."

"Oh, so you don't mind going with me alone just the two of us?"

I know he ain't trying to Mack. Please.

"Oh, no I'm good. I met your girl the other day."

He had a feeling she would say something to that effect.

"Sweet heart, I'm single. I hang with who I wanna hang with."

Umph.

"Well, take ol' girl from the studio. I'm good. Now if you will excuse me."

To let him know that there was no hard feelings, she punched him on the arm, smiled and ran up the stairs.

Although it would have been so grand to go see her favorite team play, she was not trying to go there with Diesel.

"Jazz." He called out.

She stopped at the top step.

"What's up?"

Bitches ain't shit but hoes and tricks played from his phone. ...

Unfucking believable!!!! Diesel thought when his phone rang.

"Nice ring tone." Jazz said and went on about her business.

Diesel cursed himself for allowing his homey boy to set his ring tone with that shit.

Whatever comes into this house belongs to me. So what I took it.

Love to hate me,

Mommy.

Chapter 8

Yay was ticked off. She knew her mother was scandalous, but she couldn't believe she did some punk ass shit like that. How about Peter and Ken was some real ass niggas? Her mom could have got her killed for the stunt she pulled. *People are going to stop taking me for a joke. What is this test Yay-Yay week? First, the white bitch at the club pulled that little stunt. Jazz call herself checking me and refusing my calls. And then this bitch going to come in my room and steal somebody else's shit.* The sounds of keys at the front door knocked Yay out of her trance. *Here comes the pill-head bitch.* She was referring to her mother. Her mother was not in the door good before Yay screamed on her.

"What's this?" Yay held up the note she left about taking the pills.

"What it say?" Her mother said, walking into the kitchen.

"You a dirty bitch."

Her mother cracked a smile.

"Who you think you get it from?" She said.

"I hope you die off them."

"If I do you won't get shit. Jazz is the beneficiary." Her mother teased.

She was lying. Jazz nor Yay or her sister was the beneficiary. Her first love is. If she died before him, he would know how much she really loved him and maybe then he will feel guilty about the way he had done her. Yes, she loved a man more than her own child. That's because she feels that Yay is the reason he stopped messing with her. If she would have had the abortion like he asked her to, he wouldn't have cut her completely out of his life.

Yay-Yay walked in her bedroom and slammed the door. She hated her mother as much as her mother hated her. Far as she could remember, her mother always treated her like she was a mistake. The only time she acted like she cared was when her aunt and uncle, Jazz's parents, where around. That's probably because she knew her aunt would get off in her ass for treating her such a way. She probably wanted to front for her sister's husband, like she was a loving and caring parent. Yay couldn't wait to snag a baller so she could move out that muthafucka. *That bitch going to miss me when I'm gone. Who the fuck going to help pay for her pills then? Who she going to come crying to when she having a withdrawal? Talking about her house... I'm the one that pays for damn near everything in this muthafucka. That bullshit CNA job barely paying her truck note.*

"I hate her..." Yay-Yay screamed.

She thought about calling Pam, but assumed that she would be babying Jazz. She was sure Jazz cried on her shoulders about what she told her happened between Peter and Sabrina. *After I stack this money, I got to get the fuck up out of here.* She snatched her cell phone off her bed and called her home girl, Paris.

"Sup, Delicious?" Pam asked.

"You still going to ol' boy's party tonight?"

"Yep. As long as you driving. I'm trying to get fucked up. No drinking and driving for me."

Yay-Yay told her that she would drive and to be ready within the next hour.

"Have a fat blunt and some drink when I get there." Yay said before she ended the call.

Yay sat there for a minute thinking about what she wanted to wear. She decided to go casual, but sexy. She took out a pair of purple skinny jeans, a white low cut silk shirt with the back out, and a pair of stilettos. There wasn't a need to take out panties or a bra, she would not be wearing neither. She got her towel and went down the hallway to go shower. After she got out the shower she applied some leave-in conditioner in her hair to give it a wet look. She then dried off, wrapped her towel around her and left out the bathroom. When she got in her room, she dropped her towel, walked over to the dresser, grabbed the Nivea lotion and then walked back over and sat on the bed and began to lotion her body. After she put lotion on her body, she reached over to grab her shirt and that's when she noticed a piece of mail that read, "Past Due."

"I'm not paying shit!" She screamed looking at the cable bill.

"Oh bitch you going to pay it." Her mother yelled back at her as she walked passed Yay's room to her room.

"No, I'm not. You better pay it out the money you made from stealing my shit."

Yay got up off the bed and walked over to her room door and snatched it open.

"Or did you take them? You fucking pill-head."

"I'd rather be a pill-head than a sloppy pussy ho. You fucked about fifty niggas. I saw your diary."

"Fuck you, fatal attraction bitch. It was just a fuck. He don't want you. Now, I saw your diary."

Her mother ran out from her bedroom and into Yay's room. They were face to face.

"No, bitch you ran him off." She told Yay. "You shouldn't have been born."

That stung. Yay's feelings were hurt, but she would never show it.

"Who is this nigga? Please tell me so I can beg him to come back and get your pill-head ass, and take you wherever the fuck he been hiding. I promise I'll be just like him and won't think twice about your crazy ass."

Yay looked her mother up and down with pity.

"Who the hell wants a pill-head to call their own." She said and chuckled.

"Watch your mouth before I fuck you up." Her mother warned.

"Fuck you. Now please get out my room; I have shit to do." Yay said.

"You disrespectful bitch." She said and slapped Yay.

Out of reflex, Yay slapped her back. It was not the first time her mother slapped her but it was the first time Yay hit her back. Her mother was in shock. The feeling Yay got out of hitting her mother gave her a rush, so she hit her again. This time she punched her in the nose causing her head to fall back. That's when the cat fight began. They were scratching and pulling hair. Kicking and cursing. After about two minutes, they both were tired. Yay stopped. Yay's mom walked back to her room. Yay immediately walked over to the mirror to exam her face. She had a few red marks on her face, but nothing a little make-up couldn't cover. I should fuck her up she said when she saw the long scare on her right breast.

****

Close to an hour later, Yay was dressed and pulling out of her parking spot. The weather was warm so she rolled with the sunroof up allowing the warm summer breeze to roam throughout her car. Yay's first stop was to pick up her home girl, P in Watts and then they were headed to Compton. When she got to P's house, Yay got out to go inside. Paris had a blunt and a glass of Patron waiting. After they smoked their blunt and finished a glass of Patron, the two divas were ready to head to the function on the West Side of Compton. The effects from the blunt and liquor put Yay in a way better mood. She was in so much of a good mood that she didn't even trip about the fact that the party was at a house; well a mini mansion. Later Yay found out that a doctor (RIP, Dr. Chavez) used to live there, but after he was killed, his folks started renting the spot out for different events.

It was so freaking crowded that Yay had to park across the street in the park; even then, she had to create her own parking spot behind another car on the grass. I hope they don't tow my shit, Yay thought as she and Paris got out the car.

"Bitch you know I don't do house parties. But-"

Paris cut her off. "It's a mansion party. Now put your baller radar on and let's snag us one with paper."

"Okayyyy..." Yay said and hit her hand to agree.

The two divas walked across the street and into the gate of the mansion. The guard that invited Paris spotted the dark brown, curvy, freaky stripper at the gate. He smiled and radioed the front gate guard to let her in. Once she and Yay were in the gate and up the steps that lead to the entrance of the mansion, the guard walked over. He greeted her with a kiss and thanked her for coming and whispered in her ear. She smiled and thanked him for inviting her. He had crush on P and was hoping that his courtesy will get him some play. He knew his looks and small bank roll wouldn't get a sexy gold digging dime like that.

 "Where's your boss?" P asked. That was her way of letting him know that she was not interested in small money. She wanted his boss is the owner of Chump Change production.

"He's out of town. He don't fuck with shit like this."

"Oh. Well this is my girl, Delicious, who I'm sure you know from the club."

He nodded to say yes. *Damn he a big black ugly nigga. Yay thought.* She then gave him a fake smile. Her smile became real when she noticed the famous, Suge Knight, the founder and CEO of Black Kapital Records and co-founder and former CEO of Death Row Records. He was standing by the waterfall talking with another dude that looked like money.

"Bitch, that's Suge?" Yay questioned.

"Sure is. Come on."

Paris grabbed her by the hand and they headed toward Suge's direction.

Yay's mission was delayed when she was pulled back by someone;

"What you doing in my hood?" The dude asked.

Yay was ready to snap on the fool until she looked up at him and noticed it was Wack.

"Boy, get your hands off me."

"You better watch your mouth. Call me Wack or Daddy. Keep boy out cha mouth when you talking to me."

"Delicious. You know him?

"P did a double take.

"Ain't that White-Girl's dude? Pimp?"

Wack mean mugged Paris for about 30 seconds before she turned her head.

"Don't be looking at her like that." Yay said with a fake attitude.

"Wack pulled Yay into his arms and began rubbing on her ass.

"Excuse you." Yay tried to move his hands.

"You know you like that, now stop playing." Wack told her. "I need to talk to you about something. You wanna make some money?"

"Delicious, you straight?" Paris asked.

She could tell Yay was feeling the nigga. Not just by the way she was unsuccessful with acting like she didn't like him. Shit, Yay talked about how she'll snatch him up from his white bitch whenever he came to the club, but she had to ask.

"Gone and do you." Wack told Paris. When Yay didn't say nothing, Paris walked off cursing to herself because she missed Suge.

Part 2

Chapter 9

"Yay-Yay"

It's been two weeks since I ran into Wack at the party over in Compton. Tell me why am I feeling this dude and he knows it? Ugh.... I can't stand him, but I am so into him, I mean, the way he walks, he has that cool ass gangster swag. And that "I ain't to be fucked with" disposition just puts the icing on the cake. I like the way he takes control over everything. He say shit like, "Aye, Delicious, put some fly shit on and come scoop a nigga. I wanna show you off." Before I can even contest, he finalizes it with, "Be here in an hour. If you are going to be late then don't bother to come!" Like, damn nigga. Like that? If I did have the guts to say something like that he would be like, "yup like that." Oh and don' t let me be talking shit. Y'all know I have a smart mouth. Wack do not play that. He will check my ass in a heartbeat. His favorite line, well one that he uses often is, "watch your muthafucking mouth, before I pop you in it." I know he ain't going to do shit. I be damn if I let a nigga hit on me, but I do shut up because I don't feel like hearing his mouth. That nigga is too much, that's why I can see how he would have a weak bitch's mind. That whit girl from the club he fuck with, she ain't nothing to him, but trailer park trash. He took her in when she moved down to L.A., she didn't have a place to go. He claimed his homeboy introduced them. He did admit although she is not his girl, and neither am I, that he did fuck the bitch from time to time. What nigga wouldn't? She ain't ugly. Plus, it's easy access; she does live with him. He said that he don't be fucking her like that because her hustle was not only stripping but fucking for money. I knew she was a ho. I asked him if she sells pussy why don't she have her own spot. And if she wasn't his girl why was he picking her up and dropping her off at the club.

"I really ain't tripping off her getting her own place. Shit she pay to stay here. If she move, she move, I ain't tripping off that either. I pick her up and drop her off because she don't have a car and she can't drive. Plus, she don't know her way around LA like that. And before you ask, I ain't letting her catch no cab. Niggas' thirsty for pussy. Nigga been done followed her and tried to do something to her. Just because I ain't attracted to her don't mean I don't give a fuck about her. "Those were his exact words. When he broke it down like that I couldn't do nothing but respect it. But what I don't respect, or should I say like, is how he be getting mad when he think I am out with another nigga. Or If I don't call him or answer his call when he calls, he be heated. But at the same time, he ain't trying to be with me, claiming that I ain't ready and that I have a lot of growing up to do. Oh and speaking of growing up, when I asked him what the deal was between him and that young chick, Sabrina, he claimed that she lied about her age. She told him she was nineteen. He said, he did not know the girl was only fifteen, if he did he would not have looked twice at her. He must be telling the truth because I been around him a lot and I haven't seen her. Me and Wack been kicking it since the night I seen him at the party. Do you know that night I saw him at the party we got a room and spent the night together. Tell me why he didn't try to fuck me? When I tried to come on to him he told me to slow down and that I was moving too fast. The problem was, he wasn't used to someone else being in control. That's why he had that white bitch. I can't stand her. I still got to pay that ho back from that stunt she pulled at the club. I wished she would have come home when I was over, hopefully get jealous, and get the wrong idea and leave and never come back.

I wanted to ask him where she was, but didn't. Again, I didn't feel like hearing his mouth. I hate when he calls me a drama queen or say that I'm immature.

Why I got be immature because I pout or ignore him when he hurts my feelings?

*He like the way I ride it.... He like the way I ride it......*Wack's playing my song. That's my cue. I got to go. Wack got me auditioning for this party these football players throwing.

* 4 minutes later*

This nigga done did it again. He got your girl Yay feeling extra emotional. Let me tell you what happen...

Ok, so I am rotating my hips to the lyrics while Wack sits in his chair wearing a pair of grey sweats and a wife beater. He was looking so damn good and wasn't even dressed. Halfway through the song, I slide out of my halter dress, turned around and bent over, grab my ankles and did my famous move... I made my ass clap. I quickly turn back around so that I could catch Wack's reaction; he had a smile on his face. I walked over to him and repeated the freaky lyrics in his ear. I then ran my hand across his chest onto his abs, that's when I noticed his ten inches staring at me. I bit my lip and looked at him seductively. I could sense that he wanted me as much as I wanted him. My goal was to satisfy both of our needs. I was scared of being rejected like the last time at the room, when I got butt naked and got on top of him but he pushed me away. This time I tried a different approach. I dropped to my knees. Normally I would look my prey in the eyes , but I did not want Wack to tell me to stop. So I am on my knees , mouthwatering; I am ready to suck him off real good. Once I did that he wouldn't resist the pussy. I pulled Wack's rock hard pipe out of his pants, bent down ready to suck it and he snatched me by the hair.

"What you doing, girl?" He asked.

Now I am embarrassed. My feelings were hurt. I wouldn't let him know. I put on a smile and said,

"It's part of the show."

The way he stared at me made me uncomfortable. I just knew he was calling me a young immature slut. Again, I played it off. I took my left hand and placed it on his chest as if I was telling him to stay put. I then used my right hand and stroked his dick. I looked in his eyes as I slowly moved my head down to begin my blow job. This time his facial expression read aggravated. I tried to ignore it. But.....

"Get up and go turn that radio off." He said.

I did what was asked of me. And right after, I walked over and picked my dress up off the ground, and slide it back over my head. I then went over to the sofa and retrieved my red pumps. After I put them on I grabbed my purse, keys and began to walk toward the front door.

"Yalanda." come here.

The nigga had the nerve to call me by my government name. He did sound sincere, but I didn't care, my feelings were crushed. I kept walking.

"So you wanna act like a kid now? That's what I'm talking about. Either you are going to be a kid or act like an adult. I ain't got time for that immature shit."

Without looking back, I throw up my middle finger.

"That's what you mad about. You mad because I won't fuck you."

I stopped in my tracks, turned around a gave that "nigga please" look. Just in case he did not know what I meant I broke it down. I went in my purse pulled out my cell and held it in the air,

"you see this? I can call any nigga I want to fuck." I then pointed at myself, "A bitch like me ain't never tripping off no dick."

I stood there to see what he was going to say. He stared at me like he was disgusted.

"Bitch get the fuck up out my house."

My heart dropped. I thought he hurt my feelings before, this time he really did. I wanted to curse him out. Call him a punk muthafucka. A white bitch lover, but Wack ain't the type of nigga you can call out of his name and get away with it. Even if I did have the courage, I wouldn't have spoken because I was sure my voice would have cracked up and I would have cried. I turned on my heels and tried my damndest to make the five steps that it took to get to his doorstep into two. "You must think I'm one of them bitch ass niggas you be fucking with" His voice was getting closer. "You better be glad I don't bust you in your muthafucking mouth."

My hand was on the knob and Wack was up on me holding the door shut. "Move please so I can get out of your house."

"Shut the fuck up. And turn around and look at me when I am talking to you."

"I don't have to look at you; you wanted me out your house now let me leave."

He grabbed me by both arms and made me turn around. We were face to face, although I refused to look at him I could feel him staring at me. Now I was beginning to feel like a punk bitch. Why I couldn't I look this fool in the eyes. I mean I only met him two weeks ago, unlike the dudes I would normally mess with, I would get good dick and money. But not with him. The nigga never offered me money. He purchased our meals the time we went to Roscoe's Chicken and Waffles and anytime I wanted drink and weed he got it, but that's it. And as you can see, he for damn sure wasn't giving me any dick. So why was I weak when it came to this smooth talking nigga?

Wack took my face in his hands gently.

"Look at me Yalanda." He spoke just above a whisper. OMG, I wanna scream from embarrassment just thinking about it. Why when I looked at the nigga in the eyes, tears fell? I know right!!!!! Like ugh! He whipped my tears gently with his thumbs.

"Stop crying."

I put my hands on top of his hands trying to remove them from my face, but he asked me to stop and I did.

"Look, man. I shouldn't even tell you this." He took a deep breath. "But if I don't I got a feeling a nigga is going to regret it. I like you man and you know that. I've been checking you out since the first day I saw you at the club. I knew you were feeling me but I also could tell by the way you would mad dogg White-Girl that you were a drama queen." He chuckled. "Look I don't like drama. I like peace. I don't wanna fuss and fight with my woman. I want a female that I can just chill with. I know once I give you this dick, you going be on a nigga."

"Whatever." I said, getting annoyed by his cockiness.

"Ain't no whatever to it. I know once I taste that shit, I'm going to be hooked on your young fine ass. I know you ain't ready to stop fucking with them square ass niggas you be messing with."

"I don't mess with nobody."

When I said that, his voice went from sincere to stern.

"Listen, don't never lie to me. I'm not a square ass nigga. You going to respect me. Keep it 100 or I will cut your ass off quick. I hate a lying bitch. Now like I said. You ain't ready to stop messing with them squares. So, do yo thang, little momma; I'm good with that. When I think you ready, I'm going to give you what we both been waiting for. Once I do that you're all mine. When I get you, I don't just want your pussy. I want your mind, body and soul." He then kissed me. His tongue tasted like sugar. I wanted to melt. I could have sworn I felt my wetness run down my leg. Damn, how can a kiss feel so good?

Chapter 10

"Jazz"

So it's a little past 2am and I couldn't sleep. And men were the reason. I go to the west wing of the mansion where the library is located. That's also Diesel's side of the house when he's home from school. I look through the African American Urban Fiction and Drama section. I passed up my seasoned authors that I loved to death: Tracy Brown and Wahida Clark, because more than likely I've read all their titles. There was a section labeled new authors on the scene. The Game Don't Love Nobody by Kre and ZipCodez: A Watts and Compton Tale by Aleta Williams were the two that grabbed my attention. I decided to read ZipCodez, because I recalled a few people at school talking about how good it was. I'm into the book. I was at the part when Lana and Debo were kicking it at the beach when the lights in the library went out.

"Hey, I'm in here." I said.

"My bad." The voice said and the light came back on.

I looked and it was Diesel. He smiled.

"It's almost three am; what are you doing still up?".

"Reading."

"What are you reading?"

He was leaning against the wall by the light.

"Some book called ZipCodez."

"That's a good book. Wait until you read the sequel."

I smiled and focused back on the page I was reading. I looked back up when Diesel walked up on me.

"Excuse you." I said to D when he took the book out my hand.

"I'm going to give it back. I just want to say something real quick."

I stared into his blue eyes. No, I wasn't admiring how breathtaking they were. I was curious to know why they were so glossy.

"You been drinking?"

He looked at me, like, where that come from, but answered yes to my question. I then lectured him about drinking a driving. I told him not only could he hurt himself, but he can hurt an innocent person.

"You right and that's my bad. I promise it won't happen again."

"That's good; now give me my book."

I cracked a smile.

Awkward stare.....

"Are you going to give me the book back or stare at me?"

"I'm attracted to you."

"Huh?"

Yes, I was in shock and that's all I could manage to say.

He added, "I think you might have a crush on me too."

He smiled and looked at me like he was awaiting for a response.

"Diesel, I'm sorry that I don't have the answer you're looking for. But, I do have a question. Where did all this come from? I mean, I've been Laurie's friend for close to two years now. Now all of a sudden...? That's weird. And I'm not buying it."

He took me by the hand.

"Get up and come sit over here with me." He said.

I got up from the recliner I was sitting in and walked with D over to the love seat. I sat down. He lay down.

"Well, aren't you comfortable?" I said, looking at his long legs on the arm of the coach while the back of his head rested on my lap.

"For some reason you make me that way. I know I haven't been around you like that, but... Look I can't explain it. Which means I have no lie to tell. I'm feeling you."

Silence.....

He looked up at me. I hoped my nose was clean.

"Are you listening?"

"Yes, I'm listening. But you didn't answer my question."

"Babe, I don't know why you. I've been wondering that all night. The day I gave you and my sis a ride to the dance studio, I was like damn she's beautiful."   "Thank you." I was trying not the blush.

"And then when I saw you with your boyfriend at my buddy's house, I was somewhat jealous. I know that's a trip. I was wondering what was wrong with me myself. I really was wondering what was wrong when I wanted to beat that fool's ass for disrespecting you. It ain't like it's the first time I heard him disrespect a woman. Jazz, I know you and your guy is going through something, so I'm going to leave the ball in your court. Just to let you know, you deserve better."

"D."

I paused.

"What's up?"

"How about that Lakers game?"

That was two weeks ago. And now I'm sitting here at the game chilling in the tenth row waiting on my man, Fisher, to come out. While I'm waiting, let me tell you what else happened during that two week time frame. My mother had been acting a little funny since that lady showed up talking that mess. If I didn't know any better, I would think that she was keeping something from me, but not my mom. She told me everything, including that she had sex with a few men for money. What else could there be? She didn't have AIDS, thank God the test came back negative. Other than that, I don't know what was wrong.

Yay-Yay and I barley spoke, which was fine with me. She needs to get over herself. Deep down, I did miss my cousin. I missed Peter too, but I was still mad about him trying to sleep with Sabrina. Okay, I know I probably shouldn't be telling y'all my business, but like my granny say, if you can't hide from God why hide from others. And plus, y'all cool. Okay... let me take a deep breathe. Okay... I... Gave... Diesel... My... Virginity... Your girl Jazz is no longer a virgin. Now, it wasn't a Love & Basketball moment, but it was a moment that I will never forget, one that I can't get back. And to be honest, I don't know if I want it back. Oh shoot. Here comes Diesel. So, I gotta tell you what happened later. I Know Right!?

****

Peter sat in his den drinking a bottle of Corona; it had been two weeks and Jazz showed no signs that she was going to forgive him. He called several times and each time she would send him to voicemail. He'd text and she would ignore them as well. Peter even went by her house only to get the door shut in his face. Her mother, Pam, told him that he needs to give her time, and maybe she would come around. He sure hoped so. Peter took a swig of his beer and chuckled to himself. *I guess it's true, you don't miss a good thing until it's gone.* Quiet as it was kept, he even missed Yay-Yah coming around. At least if she was around, her good-good would give him a temporality relief, but hell no. He wasn't that weak. Yay-Yah was the reason that Jazz was mad at him. If her hating ass didn't open up her mouth, he would still have his boo around. On the real though, he could have and would have looked past the stunt Yay-Yah pulled if: one, he knew for sure that Jazz would give him another chance and two, he promised Kendrick that he wouldn't fuck with her anymore. No Jazz, no Yay and no Kendrick. Kendrick was out of town putting that West Coast Fire on the map. Therefore, Peter was alone with a pocket full of money, no one to hang with or talk to about his problems. Then it dawned on him, he was going to call his nigga, Wack. The two only talked a few times since that night and Wack seemed pretty cool. Peter liked his style. He kind of looked up to Wack as a role model.

*****

When Peter got in touch with Wack he told him that he needed to get out the house, get fucked up, and blow a few stacks.

"What's up with you?" Wack questioned.

"My bitch left me." Pete said flatly.

Wack laughed. Square as nigga, he thought.

"Alright, nigga. Meet me at the Hollywood Casino. We'll fuck around there for a minute and then hit Starz."

Peter smiled at Wack's suggestions. Despite the way they met, Peter believed it happened for a good reason. He found somebody that was down with gambling and splurg'n on pussy.

"The casino and the strip club? It's about time I found somebody down to live life. That nigga Ken would never..."

Wack cut him off.

"Don't talk about your boss." Wack teased.

"Ain't no boss. We both bosses. One don't run the other."

"I can't tell. But, anyway. I'll meet you at the Casino. Let me get rid of this bitch."

"Alright. Is an hour good?"

Wack told him that an hour would be fine. He then walked back into the living room and told Yay that he would hook up with her later. Yay's mood had changed from vulnerable to upset. She was frowning up at the TV like she had a problem with the Lakers winning.

"Damn, shorty, it ain't that serious. I ain't no Lakers fan either, but shit I don't let them get to me."

Wack hit her on the arm to get her attention. She looked up and gave a fake smile.

"I'm about to head to the club." "Call me later" She said, still looking at the TV.

"That's cool, but what's wrong with you?"

"Besides seeing my shady ass cousin in the audience with my ex, nothing." Yay lied.

Well she did see D and J at the game, but D was far from her ex. They never had no type of relations. She only saw him once and his attention was on White-Girl.

"You see, niggas ain't the only ones who are shady. Bitches is too. But on the real, don't let that ho ruin your night. Go make that money."

He pulled her to him,

"You still got feelings for the nigga?"

"Hell no. I dumped him. I'm just mad that she would go behind me and mess with somebody I had." She got carried away with her lie, "I was pregnant by him. But anyway, fuck him and her too," she said. "I'm trying to be with you."

"In due time, ma, in due time." He kissed her on the forehead. She reached up and kissed his lips. Wack was the first one to pull away.

"Get to work he told her."

She left.

****

Later On...

Peter and Wack sat in the bar area drinking on XO, barley making small talk because the Lakers and the Heat game was on. Kobe had just hit a three and tied the game up, right before half time.

"Bet one, the Lakers take it." Peter challenged Wack.

He had just learned Wack wasn't a Lakers fine.

"I ain't got it like that right now. That's why I'm up here. Shit. A nigga hoping they win something."

Wack took a sip from his drank.

"On the real, I'm hoping you can front a nigga a stack or two. My hand itching. I know I'm going to hit."

He looked at Peter for a response.

"Yeah, whatever," Peter said.

Wack looked up at him and noticed the game had his attention. It was half time so what they fuck was he looking at? Fucking weirdo, Wack thought.

"Man you gon' let a nigga get two stacks. I'm about to break the house?"

Wack got up from the bar.

"And why in the fuck you sitting here looking like a sad puppy."

"I don't mean to be acting like that, but I saw my ex-girl on T.V. with a white boy."

"At the game?"

Wack asked, looking up at the T.V.; he wondered if these were the same people that Yay saw on T.V.

"Yeah." Peter answered.

"Oh, well, get over that shit. It's plenty bitches out here. Now let me hold that."

Wack looked at the clock.

He was anxious. The casino staff had just did a shift change. Wack had a theory that you had better chances at winning when the dealer first started the shift. Peter reached in his pocket and handed Wack the two stacks he asked for.

"Good looking out."

Wack said and walked away.

★★★★★★★★★★★★★★★

Nigga say what?

Loaded off that liquid courage and pockets phatter than they were before he made it to the casino, Peter was feeling himself.

"Don't never disrespect me like that. Do it look like I need security. Gon' with that bullshit."
That's how Peter got at the casino security when they offered to escort him out the casino.

"Wuts up?" Wack said, as he approached the trio. *This nigga tripping, he thought, when he noticed the mug on Peter's face.*

"Man these two niggas talking about do I need them to escort me to my car. Fuck I look like. I'm a gangster."

Since when? Wack thought.

"Oh, nigga, you hit?" Wack asked playing off like he didn't know.

"Yeah, twelve racks. You can keep that two I gave you. I ain't hurting."

"That's what's up. Good looking out." Wack replied.

"Come on let's roll."

Peter looked at the guards.

"Oh fake ass man in black." Peter dissed before him and Wack walked out the casino to their separate cars. They would meet up at Starz; it was ten minutes away.

When Pete and Wack got in their rides, they both picked up there cell phone.

"En route" Wack told the goon on his line. Without exchanging any other words, him and the goon ended their call.

"I saw you and that busta ass white boy on T.V.; that's how you do huh? That's cool. I still love you." That was the message Peter left Jazz.

He then called Yay-Yay.

"What the fuck you want?" Is how she answered the phone.

"I need some pussy. And I know you need your car note paid. I'm about to come to the club. Be prepared to leave with me. Oh, and I'm doing it VIP style. So you and your clique be prepared to entertain me and my boy."

Yay looked at the phone and rolled her eyes. She put it back on her ear.

"First off nigga, don't come at me like..." she stopped in the middle of her sentence when she heard a baritone voice telling Peter to break himself.

"Give me that right there."
The goon was talking about the black bag that Wack told him Peter's money was in.

Any other time, Peter would have gave up the money with no problem, but the liquid courage wouldn't let him do it.
"Fuck you nigga." Peter said and pushed out. Peter didn't even get a good twelve feet away before he lost control of his car. His car flipped over two times before landing into a bus stop bench.
"Damn. Wack said out loud.
He reached in his astray, pulled out a half of blunt, lit it up, and waited a few minutes before he would go check on Peter. The bystanders that looked in shock knew for a fact that whoever was in the car was gone.

"Rest in peace." Were the thoughts of the basket pusher before he continued on his recycle mission.
"Peter what the fuck? Peter are you there? PETER!" Yay didn't get a response.

"Jazz"

"Shot, shot, shot, shot!" Laurie and Diesel screamed. We were in the den playing truth or dare. On my turn I landed on dare and it was Laurie's crazy ass turn to dare me.

"I dare you to run down the street in your panties and bra and scream five dollars."

She and I both laughed. Diesel didn't think it was funny. Laurie and I did, because only she would come up with something like that, and we both knew I wasn't going to do it. So of course I had to take a shot. We played for an hour straight before I threw up the white flag. I was tow up and not trying to drink anymore. Laurie was so drunk that Diesel had to carry her to her room. I undressed her for him and tucked her under the covers. Before I left out, I put a trash can by her bed, just in case she threw up. After that, I grabbed my towel and walked into Laurie's bathroom to shower. When I came back in the room from my shower, Laurie was complaining about her head hurting. With my towel wrapped around me I made my way to the hallway closet where they kept the medicine.

"Just what the doctor ordered."

I smiled at the voice behind me and chills ran through my body from the kiss Diesel planted on the back of my neck. Diesel continued planting small sensual kisses behind my ear, which made me wet. With my eyes closed, light moans escaped from my mouth. It took all the will power I had to muster up what I was about to say.

"Please. Don't do this to me. I need to take your sister her medicine."

Diesel turned me around and gently pulled my face up and kissed me. I wanted to melt in his hands. I don't know how, but my towel ended up on the hallway floor and Diesel was on his knees, holding both of my breast in one hand, licking on my nipples, and with the other he was playing with my pierced pearl tongue. "Oh my goodness, baby. It feels soooo good." I moaned.

Diesel then took his mouth off my nipples and began squeezing each one with the tip of his fingers. Still messaging my clit, he worked his tongue from my belly button down to my clit and replaced his fingers with his tongue.

"Oh shit, Diesel."

My head went back in pure bliss as he fucked me with his tongue. It didn't take long for me to get weak in the knees. It was feeling so good. I started squeezing his shoulder with one hand and rubbing in his hair with the other. And then I couldn't take it anymore. I let out a loud scream. I thought I was going to collapse, but Diesel held me up. He got up from his knees, wiped his mouth, picked me up and kissed me. Diesel carried me into his room on the other side of the mansion and laid me on his bed. He stared at me with a warm smile. I nodded my head at how sexy he is.

"Come here." I told him.

"For what?" He asked.

I don't know if I meant it at the time or I was saying what I thought I was supposed to say; whatever my reason was, I couldn't and wouldn't take it back.

"I want you to make love to me."

He stared at me with those deep blue eyes. He bit his bottom lip.

"Are you sure?"

I nodded my head yes.

I watched him as he undressed. He took off his shirt first. Baby body was bagging. He then pulled off his pants and then his boxers. He definitely inherited his tool from the black side of his family. He reached in his drawer and grabbed a condom. My heart was beating fast as I watched him put the condom on. I was nervous and anxious for what was about to happen next, all at the same time. For the first 15 to twenty minutes I was in pain, but after that I was working my hips like a belly dancer. Damn it felt good. Diesel repped the song well *"he got a big dick and he know how to use it."* Y'all probably thinking what I know being that he's my first. I know I had over four orgasms and one time it squirted out like a waterfall. Like I said, my first wasn't a Love & Basketball moment, but he was just right for me.

"Excuse me miss. Excuse me." That's Peter's nurse. She came to go over his aftercare. After being in the hospital for a week, he is finally being released. Peter doesn't have any family; his mother is dead and he never knew his father. Ken and I are the only ones that he considers family. Since Ken is out of town and can't make it back until Saturday, Peter is under my care. I bet you all are wondering what happened to Diesel. Well the night D and I was seeing the Lakers game, Yay called and told me that she was at the scene where Peter was in a bad accident. Somebody tried to rob him. She told me that they were rushing Peter to the hospital and that people said they don't think he was going to make it. I panicked. I mean, I was really hyperventilating. Luckily, there were medical people at the game that helped me calm down. I was given a brown paper bag and was told to take deep breaths in it. Once I was calm, I told D what happened. His mouth said one thing, "Do you want me to take you to the hospital?" But the look on his face said another, "I know the fuck she ain't doing all that over this nigga." That pissed me off. Without saying a word, I jumped up and walked as fast as I could out of the game. D was right behind me. I stood at the exit of the Staples Center, pulled out my phone and called my mom. I wasn't getting in the car with his selfish, jealous ass. D stood there and listened while I told my mother what happened and that I needed her to pick me up. She asked where D was, and I told her he was standing next to me, but I didn't want him taking me. D cracked a smile at that part, and I snapped

,

"I don't see what's so damn funny."

"Your childish, confused ass is real funny." He reached in his pocket, pulled out a napkin and threw it to me. "Go blow your nose." He said, and walked back into the game. I couldn't believe him. I told my mother; she understood his actions. She said that he was hurt and jealous. "Jazz, if you still loved Peter and you knew that you didn't want to be with Diesel or have feelings for him like that, why did you give him you?" At that moment I didn't have an answer. At that moment I was worried about Peter. At the moment, I regretted what happen between D and I. As the week went by and Peter was doing well, I wanted to make things right with D and I needed him to fill the void I had in mine. But every time I called, he sent me to voicemail. Laurie said she wasn't in it and in the same breath she suggested that I let him be and stay with Peter. She didn't have to say it, but I knew she didn't trust me with her brother's heart. I wondered if D was missing me like I was missing him and hoped that he had not moved on.

Chapter 12

"Wack"

Pow! I back handed my white bitch so hard she flew over the back of the couch. I looked at her while she lay on the floor holding a bloody lip. I walked over to her, and grabbed her by her hair. I stared into her blue eyes. I had to let her know that I was serious. The shit that she helped me do was between me and her only.

"If you ever tell anybody about what went down, I'll kill you bitch. Your my ho; I own you. You got that?"   She nodded her head yes.

"Now go clean your face. Roll me up a goodie and run me a hot bath."

I walked over to the kitchen counter and took a swig from the Remy bottle. I cut my eyes at my snow bunny. She was going inside the duffle bag.

"Fuck you in there for?"

"I rolled the last of what we had before we left today." She said nervously.

"So you trying to tell me that I smoked up a pound of powder? Bitch you playing with me."

I walked over to where she was and pushed her down on the couch.

"You fucking with my shit?"

"No babe, I haven't. I don't mess with that stuff."

I laughed.

"Bitch you saying that stuff like it's a bad thing. Oh you too good to fuck with it?"

"Wack I told you how I feel about drugs. Drugs destroyed my family." She started to cry.

I knew what I was about to make her do was fucked up, but ain't no way a bitch of mines gon' think she better than me. I snatched the bag of pure coke out of the bag. I then walked over to the kitchen counter, grabbed a knife and walked back over to where she was sitting. I tossed the bag of coke on the coffee table, and slid a chair up to the table. After I sat down, I looked at my snow bunny.

"What the fuck you crying for? You don't trust me? How in the fuck you don't trust the man you claim you love?"

She did not say nothing.

I stabbed the knife in the coke bag and then proceeded to cut the package open.

"This nigga got this shit sealed up tight." I thought to myself.

Thinking about Debo made me more pissed than I already was. The anger I had toward Debo gave me the strength to cut the bag open. Once the bag was open, I got the weed, some zig zags, and a couple of pinches of coke. I rolled up one of my special joints. I handed it to White-Girl.

"You know what to do, I told her.

Part 4

Chapter 12

Skeletons

"So, you fucking the pastor now?" Pam looked at Calvin in shock. She then looked at the biracial couple on her left. They didn't hear. She looked over at the Latino family on her right and all eyes were on her. "Oh, so now y'all muthafuckas understand English?" She screamed on the family and then rolled her eyes. She looked at Calvin.

"Don't come at me with no bullshit your momma done filled your head with." she told him.

"My momma ain't told me shit. If she knew you and that nigga was fucking, she would have been got at you and that nigga too."

He had a point. So if Mrs. Lewis didn't tell him, then it had to be her sister who told. And no, she wasn't fucking the Pastor. Yeah, they had been on a few dates that's about it, but he was the perfect gentlemen. He never tried to touch Pam. Although, she kind of wanted him to.

"I'm not fucking him. If I was, then I would tell you. Why the fuck not? What I got to lose? I'm dying any mother fucking way!"

Calvin ran his hand across his forehead. He stopped at the temple and massaged it.

"You're not dying; you're just as, if not healthier, than people who don't have the virus."

"Anyway, I came here because you haven't called. I need $6000.00 for Jazz's party."

"SIX!" Calvin raised his voice. Remembering he was in a facility where a bunch of cock strong guards were that was waiting to run up on inmates and beat them down,

he lowered his voice.

"What type of party is this? I'm not spending that type of money on a party. I'm going to get her a car. You want to give her a party, you do it. Don't you got niggas?"

"No, I don't have niggas. I have clients. The money I make from them is to take care of bills. It's not their job to take care of your child. Damn, that's the least you can do."

The two debated for a few more minutes until Calvin gave in. Calvin told Pam that he would send his boy to drop off the money.

"Thanks Bae. And for real, I'm not sleeping with no one for pleasure. I love you!"

Pam was telling the truth. Although she enjoyed sex with two of her clients, she wasn't doing it for pleasure. And yes, she did love Calvin. Why else would she be with a man that is the cause of her having HIV?

"I love you too. Now tell me what's up with you and the pastor. Pam don't fucking lie to me."

This nigga must think I'm stupid. Does he honestly think I'm going to tell him that this pastor guy gives me the chills? That I often wondered what it would be like to be the first lady? Hell no. I'm not going to tell him that! Besides, ain't nothing going to ever happen with me and the pastor. What he want with me?

"Calvin, if I was interested in the man, what is the chance that he and I will work out? I'm a ho with HIV."

Calvin stared into Pam's deep brown eyes. He saw disappointment, regret, and pain. He was used to seeing everything but happiness in Pam's eyes. He hated what he allowed to happen to her. He hated that she loved him so much that she put her life on the line for him. He would never admit to himself, or anyone else, that he was glad the virus made her insecure. He knew for a fact that she wouldn't leave him for no reason, not for his infidelity.

"Baby smile; you're scaring me." Calvin told Pam.

She gave a weak smile.

"It's going to be alright. You're tougher than that HIV shit." He told her.

"Yeah, whatever

"Pam"

After I leave the prison from seeing my husband, I head to my sister's house. I'm about to put the hater in her place. How dare she go back and tell Calvin anything about me; what's the purpose? I understand her and Calvin are like sister and brother; they were always cool, but I'm her flesh and blood. How many times do I have to get it through her fucking head? I pull up to the projects where her and my niece reside, park, pop my truck and retrieve my tennis shoes. Yes, I was getting prepared to whip my sister's ass. She has a smart mouth, don't like to admit when she's wrong, and is scary as hell. After I put on my shoes, I bail to the door. I did not come in peace so why pretend.

Boom Boom Boom. "Open this muthafucking door."

"Who is that?" I hear my niece say.

 "It's your aunt; now come open the door."

When Yay opened the door, the first thing she asked after giving me a once over is:

"What my momma do?"

She then stepped to the side and let me in. Ignoring the question,

I asked, "Where is she?"

"I'm not sure, auntie. I heard her on the phone asking was her pictures ready."

I made my way up the steps and into her room. She wasn't there. I had an idea.

"Hey, Yay. Go move my car to another building. I wanna surprise her when she came back. I gave Yay my keys, went back in my sister's room and sat on the chair next to her bed.

I don't deserve this shit. I thought.

Flashback -Fifteen Years Ago

"Hey, boo; I'm about to make some Tacos." Pam said to Calvin as she walked past him toward the kitchen.

"Where that blunt at you had?" He asked, never taking his eyes off the TV.

"I smoked it nigga, what you think?"

"Damn, you didn't bother to see if I wanted to hit it or not! Fuck, Cuz, damn!"

He threw the PS controller at the T.V. He then got up and walked toward the entertainment center, took a CD out the case and put it in the player. Tupac's Gangster Party blasted throughout the house. The music was way too loud, but in the projects it was the thing to do. In the projects nobody ever slept.

Pam didn't come out of the kitchen until she finished preparing the tacos. She was so glad Jazz was at her grandmother's house, although she didn't like the old bitch. She hated when Jazz was around and Calvin would flip. Calvin had been acting funny lately, real moody. She already knew what the problem was, his money was funny. He wasn't getting it like he was before she had Jazz and when his brother was alive. They used to have their hands in any and everything illegal. Home invasions were their specialty. Now that his brother was dead, he had nobody to watch his back, since a snitch is the reason his brother was killed. A snitch from their hood; he didn't trust nobody. Pam didn't want Calvin going out there doing shit that would cause him to go to jail, so she came up with an idea. She was getting a job. She didn't tell him but she had been putting in applications everywhere. Church's Chicken was one place that wouldn't call her back. The manager was a bitch she went to high school with. The chickenhead, tramp used to spread rumors about her. Claiming that she was a toss-up, Calvin confronted Pam about the rumors, but he refused to tell her who said it. He finally gave in when Pam wouldn't talk to him for a week. He lied and told her ol' girl said it. After Pam stomped her out, Pam found out from her friend Stacy that it was her sister that told it. Pam beat her sister's ass too. They both deserved it. Any bitches that showed hate deserved getting they ass beat.

"Here you go, baby." Pam said and handed Calvin his tacos.

She couldn't hear him because the music was blasting, but she read his lips. He said thank you. She watched him while he ate. She always did. He had no problem with it. After he finished eating, she wiped his mouth, cleaned his hands with the towel she had, and removed his tray. After she cleaned the dishes, she went to shower. When she got out the shower, she put on one of Calvin's wife beaters, tying it up in the front, showing off her belly button and lace thong. After Pam finished with her final touches: perfume, body spray and lip gloss, she went in her secret stash and fired up her special joint. Calvin would have beat her ass if he knew she was fucking with primos. It was a habit she picked up in middle school, compliments of her best friend, Stacy. After three pulls she was straight. She sprayed the bathroom and walked out and into their bedroom. Calvin was playing Adina Howard's T-Shirt and Panties; he knew she loved the artist.. He also knew just hearing the song would put Pam in a creative mood. And it did. She put her 4 inch red pumps on. She was now ready to put on a show for her man. The music and her special joint gave her so much confidence. Dancing was what she loved to do, but Calvin wasn't having it. He went off when he found out her and her friend, Stacy auditioned for a strip club. Later, he would change his mind. Until then... she was Nicety... That's the name Calvin gave her. He said she was a nice, but nasty freak. Nicety was so high it felt like she was flying. She felt even sexier than she looked. She stepped into the living room with her back turned toward Calvin. She began moving in slow motion; like a sexy ballerina. As she twirled around, she pulled her shirt up over my head and tossed it in the air. She then bent forward, placing her hands on her calves and moved her ass up and down; popping it just right to the rhythm. After shaking her ass for a few more minutes, she stood back up. Her back still toward Calvin, she did a little twirl with her head, and with one hand she unclamped her barrette and her long brown hair fell to her ass. She turned around, pulled down her thong, and strutted toward her man to feed it to him.

"Oh my gosh." She screamed in fear. There were two big black dudes in her living room. One had a gun pointed at Calvin and the other was punching him in the face. From what she could see, blood was everywhere. Without thinking, or even caring that she could be shot, she charged at the man that was using Calvin's face for a punching bag.

"Get off him you fat fuck." The man that was holding the gun snatched Pam by the hair, and threw her up against the entertainment system. Whatever she hit when she hit the radio caused it to cut off. Pam laid there for a minute. She wasn't in pain, thanks to the laced joint she hit, but she was trying to register what happened. The dude that was punching Calvin stopped and looked at Pam with a wicked smile.

"You love your nigga?" He asked her.

She was now sitting up, looking at Calvin. She ignored the man.

"Calvin baby are you okay?" She said, getting up as she held her back.

"Bitch, don't move." The gunman warned.

Pam ignored him too. She walked slowly over toward Calvin and wrapped her arms around his neck. "Get him an ambulance now." Both of the bears laughed.

"Bitch I call the shots." The one that was punching Calvin said. "Now I want my mutha fucking money."

"What money? Calvin what is he talking about?"

The guy that was holding the gun walked over to Calvin and Pam and tried pulling her off. She held her grip around Calvin's neck.

"You fat bitch; let me go." She cried.

"Bam." He slapped her.

"Watch your mouth when you talk to a man."

"Man, leave her alone. I'm going to get you your money!"

"And how is that?" The boss man asked.

Calvin begged for the two big black men to give him 24hours to come up with a plan. They agreed. They knew the nigga couldn't get far within twenty-four hours. When they left, Pam ran and locked the door. She wanted to call the police, but knew that was a no no from where she come from. Besides, what would they do? The next day, Pam and Calvin went down to the owner's place of business - The booking joint on 85th and Vermont. Calvin told him that Pam and him needed at least 30 days to pay the debt. After explaining how they was going to get the money: working at the strip club and after hours he owned, the owner smiled. Not because Pam's fine ass would make him lots of money, he was pleased. But not as pleased as he would be by sticking his dick in her. He looked at Calvin,

"Do you wanna stick around while I test my product?"

"Test who. Nah nigga, you ain't fucking my girl?"

The boss went under his desk and pulled out his Beretta. He aimed at Calvin.

"Does that mean you have my $3000.00 deposit?"

"You didn't say I gotta give you a deposit. I ain't got $3000.00. Besides, I only you $4000.00."

"Nah, you owe me $6000.00. Nigga, interest."

He cocked his gun, aimed at Calvin's knee and shot him. Calvin yelled in pain, Pam screamed in fear.

"I'll do whatever you want please don't kill him."

"Pam shut the fuck up."

Calvin spoke through clenched teeth.

"You ain't fucking that nigga."

Pow! He shot Calvin in the arm.

"Please stop. I'll do whatever you want." Pam cried.

By this time, Calvin was sweating and blood was dripping everywhere. He needed to get to a hospital quick. And Pam knew that they wouldn't let them leave until she did what they wanted. She quickly stripped out of her clothes, and stood there. The boss man stroked his rock hard dick.

"Come around here." He ordered. "Get on your knees."

Pam almost gagged when she saw his dick. There were bumps all over it.

"What's that?" She said pointing at his disgusting looking tool.

"An almond joy. Now SUCK IT!"

Pam closed her eyes and imagined she and Calvin was making love on their honeymoon. Putting herself in another place always worked when she used to have sex with her mother's boyfriend. Pam always was the one that suffered just to make sure the ones she loved was alright! She did it for her sister; she refused to allow her mother's man to sleep with her baby sister. Now she was doing it for her husband. Pam sucked and sucked on the nasty penis. You would have thought the old bastard would have nutted quick, but he didn't.

"Get on the table." He ordered Pam.

Pam got up. She made sure she didn't look at Calvin. She didn't want to see the disappointment in his eyes. Little did she know Calvin was taken to the back to get medical treatment from the boss' hoe; she was an RN.

"I want it from the back." He told Pam.

Pam got on all fours and he rammed himself inside of her. It didn't hurt, but it felt disgusting. He fucked Pam and emptied his semen in her.   Once Calvin was stitched up, he was wheeled from the back in a wheelchair. Who knows where the chair came from? By the time he made it to the front, Pam was dressed. She looked for Calvin, but he wasn't there. Before she could ask where he was at, she saw him in the wheelchair. She ran over to him and hugged him.

"Baby you ok?" She asked.

He didn't say nothing.

"Get them out of here." The boss ordered. The bodyguard grabbed Pam by the arm and the RN wheeled Calvin out. Once the four made it to the car, the bodyguard threw Calvin in the van first, then Pam.

"Drive them home. Be back in twenty minutes. Don't make me come after you." He warned the RN.

He then turned to Pam, "you be at the club by 4pm tomorrow. If you late, that's your ass." He then laughed. "Don't be mad at me, be made at this nigga." He pointed at Calvin and then turned and walked off.

As soon as Pam and Calvin made it to their apartment,

Pam ran and got Calvin some pain killers and a glass of whiskey to wash it down. She then took a hot shower. She scrubbed and scrubbed, both her body and her mouth. After she was done, she ran Calvin a bath. When she came out he was gone. Her gut told her that something bad happened. She didn't find out until three days later.

Calvin confessed that he killed both of the guys and the girl. They both hugged and cried on each other's shoulders. That wouldn't be the end of their tears.

It was 12:00am when Pam got up to go to the bathroom. She pulled her panties down and sat on the toilet. She screamed so loud when the urine touched the raw parts of her vagina. Calvin snatched both his guns and kicked in the bathroom door, ready to kill whoever. He looked around and didn't see anyone. He looked at Pam. Tears ran down her face.

"Baby I think he gave me something."

She looked down at her swollen, bumpy coochie. Calvin couldn't believe his eyes. The coochie that was once a pretty sight to see, was now the most disgusting thing he ever saw.

"You did fuck him?" Calvin said in disbelief.

He thought he saw her sucking his dick when he was being carried out the room, but he was not for certain. Now he was not only sure that she did suck it, but she fucked him. That wasn't part of the plan.

The next day Pam and Calvin went to the doctor. She was diagnosed with herpes on the spot. Seven days later, her test results came back and she tested positive for HIV. She and Calvin never told anyone. Calvin felt so guilty. He told her not to fuck him. He didn't think she loved him that much, but she did. He loved her too. They loved each other, but will that change when Pam finds out the truth?

The sounds of her ringing cell phone brought Pam out of her trance. Pam looked at her cell and smiled. It was the pastor.

"Hi." She answered.

"Hey there." He responded.

His voice was so deep and sexy. It fit him perfect. Pastor Ron is 50 years old, but don't look a day over thirty. He is dark skin, medium build, with nice arms and abs. He wears a low cut and has a goatee . He is what you call, a man. A sexy one at that. She met him one day when he came to see Jazz perform.

"How are you, baby girl?"

Pam couldn't believe she was blushing off of a hi, how are you, baby girl. She wondered what she would do if the man touched and kissed her.

"I'm fine. Now that you called."

He chuckled a little bit.

"That's good to hear. I called to invite you to breakfast tomorrow morning."

"I would love to." She said.

"That's great. I have a meeting. I will call you later if it's not too late."

"K!"

He said good bye first, and then Pam. When Pam hung up with the Pastor, she had a smile on her face that could light the darkest alley. She was no longer thinking about her illness. Her pastor friend told her, *if Satan can steal your joy, then he has you right where he wants you.* That's what he was trying to do, get Pam where he wanted her: back to being insecure, and unhappy with her life. That's why when her past tried to tell her that there was no hope for a better future, she would rebuke it in the name of Jesus. She walked over to her sister's dresser, looked in the mirror, smiled and said, "I am somebody. I am a child of God. I will not allow no one or nothing make me doubt that God loves me." That was something else she learned from her pastor friend. It seemed as if the man always knew what she was thinking, or feeling. She wished she would have met him fifteen years ago. She glanced down at the dresser and shook her head at the five different pill bottles. She wasn't a saint herself, she did the coke from time to time, but she didn't think she was an addict like her sister. Pam admired the dark red and pink colors on the Bible that sat on the dresser. Woman, Thou Art Loosed, by TD Jakes; Pam was impressed. She did not have a clue that her sister even knew what a Bible was. Pam picked it up, and opened it. Pam smirked at what it said on the dedication page: *To the daughter I never had from Mrs. Lewis.* Calvin's mother gave her the Bible. Pam flipped through the pages. She noticed a small white envelop; she knew that CRC stamp anywhere. It was prison mail. She picked up the envelope. It was addressed to her sister from her husband. *What the hell he writing her for?*

Pam opened the letter and what she read caused her to burst into tears. *How could she, how could they? Oh my God!*

Part 5

Chapter 13

"Jazz"

Three days after Peter was released from the hospital, he had to appear in Inglewood court. The hospital staff reported to the Inglewood Police Department that the accident was caused by him

being under the influence. They said his alcohol level was way over the approved amount for a person operating a vehicle. The fact that his life was in danger did not matter. All they were focused on was him drinking and driving. Prejudice, if you ask me. Peter was going to fight it, but his attorney told him that it was best that he take a deal, which is six months house arrest, licensed suspended for a year and one hell of a fine. If he would have taken it to trial, he would have had to serve a year in the county, plus the above; if he lost. He asked me what should he do; I told him to take the deal too. If he lost, he would be in a cell with two broken legs; at least being out he would be more comfortable with the cast and still have his freedom in the comfort of his own home.

"I may as well go to jail. At least I will have some help." Peter whined.

"Not the help you need. Them people won't give you the proper care you need. It's dirty and everything in there. And what you mean, at least you will have help? Haven't I been by your side since day one? You know me and Ken got your back." I explained.

He smiled. He acted like that was the main reason he did not try to fight it in trial. I did not mind stepping in and supporting him emotionally, and helping out when his nurse wasn't around. I care for

Peter. But the more I was around Peter, the more I realized he was no longer the man that I wanted to spend my life with. I loved Peter, but more in a friend kind of love. I wanted and needed Diesel. I wanted to tell him that I was sorry for the way that I acted at the game, and that Peter was just a friend that I was helping out. I wanted to let him know that he was the one I wanted, not Peter. But, yeah right. He would not understand that I was practically staying at Peter's house because Ken was out of town and he had no one else to help him. He wouldn't understand that I would sometimes make runs for Peter because he couldn't drive, and that the only reason why I was doing it is to help him keep his clientele. At least I was getting paid for it; right?

Malibu, CA

When Jazz arrived at the Malibu beach-front home of Arizona draft pick, M.J. Sanders, she was a little excited. She may not be a fan of football, and did not know what he looked like, but the fact that he was a celebrity sent butterflies through her stomach. She cut the engine, took the keys out, and reached over to unlock the glove compartment. She grabbed the Ziploc bag that was filled with X pills and placed it in her Dior bag. She closed the glove compartment back. This time, she did not lock it. She sat up in her seat, cut the dome light on for light in the car and adjusted the rearview mirror. Jazz went in her purse and pulled out her compact and lip gloss. Looking in the rearview mirror, she touched up her make-up. When she was done, she put the make-up back in her purse and pulled out her Tommy Girl perfume. She sprayed a little behind each ear and some in her hair. She was now ready to go handle business. She got out of Peter's 745, hit the alarm and walked to the door. She never noticed the masked gunman sitting in the car behind her.

Ding dong ....was the sound of the doorbell. Jazz smiled at the guy that answered the door.

He was a short, stocky, dark skin guy with waves and a nice smile. If he wasn't Sander's, she was sure he was a ball player.

"Hello, I'm Jazz. I got that West Coast Fire." She said nervously.

The dude smiled and looked behind him. He grabbed her by her arm to escort her in the house. They got it turned up, Jazz thought, looking at everybody enjoying themselves. There were people smoking weed,

taking shots, playing cards, and dancing; everyone was having a good time.

"That West Coast Fire is in the building. "The guy that answered the door announced. Damn, like that? She thought. The nigga is a straight pill-head. The dude then whispered in Jazz's ear. "This fool crazy", she thought. She reached up and touched his shoulders. He leaned his head down so she could say what she had to say.

"I'm not the stripper. I came to deliver that West Coast Fire." Is Denzel here? Denzel, he repeated and scrunched up his eyebrows. Then he remembered; she must be talking about Diesel. Jazz was asked to ask for a Denzel or another person, but she forgot his name.

"Oh, I know who you are talking about." he said.

He took Jazz by the hand and walked her toward a crowd of dudes that where making a bunch of wolf sounds. The guy pulled her through the crowded hallway, and that's when she saw him, that's when she saw them. The white girl, Savanna, was butt naked dancing on a guy who looked identical to the guy that answered the door. And then there was the biracial Justin Timberlake look alike, pouring champagne on a naked light skin tramp's ass cheeks and licking it off. Jazz was in shock. It really did not bother her to see the white girl, but seeing Diesel and Yay-Yay put on a freak show, was not was she expected or wanted to see. The dude that answered the door went over to Diesel and told him what was up.

Chapter 14

When Diesel looked up and saw Jazz standing there staring at him in shock, he felt bad. He pushed Delicious out of the way, got up off his knees and made his way to Jazz. "Hey." He said, while trying to grab her hand, but she snatched away. "You are no different than the rest of them." She said. "Let me talk to you." Diesel made another attempt to grab her hand and again she snatched away. He looked into her eyes. Her eyes said that I thought you were different. Her eyes said that you are pathetic. Her eyes said that she refused to allow her tear drops to fall. He wanted to hold her and tell her that he was sorry. That it was not what it looked like, and that he was just having some fun to get her off his mind. The tension was so thick between the two you could cut it with a knife. To everyone that was looking, it was obvious that the two shared chemistry.

"What's up D?" The guy that answered the door said. "You going to get it or what?" He asked.

"Get what?" An aggravated D asked.

"That West Coast Fire? She delivering it." He said, pointing at Jazz.

D looked at Jazz. He was pissed off. He couldn't believe that he had been played again. Here he was feeling bad about what she just witnessed and she risking her life for another nigga. For the same nigga that she went off on him about and left him at the Staple game because he did not give a damn if her ex lived or died. He felt like a sucka. He allowed his heart to give love another try just for her. He spent money on her. He took her out to the finest restaurants and splurged on her one Saturday at the Grove. He shared things with her that he never shared with his sister or mother because he did not want them to view him as weak. Yeah, it had only been three weeks but D knew his heart, he was in love with a seventeen year old. D went in his pocket, and pulled out a few big faces; as he was handing her the money, he asked, "You got the pills?" Jazz's hands shook as she went in her bag to pull out the pills. She knew D was upset and she was ashamed about the foolish act that he found out about. When she pulled out the bag of pills, D wanted to call her stupid and slap her ass across the room. Without looking at D, she passed him the bag. He gave it to his homey. D didn't pop; he purchased the product as a treat for the guest that came out. During this time White-Girl and Delicious was getting an eye full. White-Girl wasn't tripping off the fact that she knew D; felt something for the little girl. She had one thing and one thing only on her mind: a come up. Yay, on the other hand, was pissed off when she saw Jazz and D make the exchange. She was about to go let them know just how pissed she was. When Yay walked up, Jazz could have killed her with her gaze. That wench knew who D was; they discussed him when Yay came to see P at the hospital. She knew that D was Laurie's brother. She also knew that he was looking to be drafted real soon. That's all she cared about when Jazz told her that she gave D her virginity. When Jazz told her cousin about the time she had been spending with D, Yay acted as if she was happy. Jazz couldn't see it then, but was sure of it now, that the chick is mad because she is her and she is who she is: a salty, grimy, envious ghetto bitch.

"Oh, so you working for Peter now? Yay-Yay said to Jazz.

With a frown on her face, Jazz looked her naked cousin up and down. and responded with a slap to Yay-Yay' jaw.
Yay held her face in shock.

"Fuck you." Jazz said.

Finally registering in Yay's brain what just happened, she swung on Jazz. Jazz ducked and came back up and went to hit her with a quick left, but missed. D grabbed Yay and the guy that answered the door grabbed Jazz, picked her up and escorted her out the house to her car. Jazz could hear Yay screaming and cursing at D to let her go. She didn't want none.

The dude did not put Jazz down until the two of them made it out the front door.

"You are too pretty to be fighting."

"So, pretty girls don't fight? They are supposed to allow people to walk all over them?

"I'm not saying that at all. D don't want that girl, she ain't nothing but a stripper."

"She's my cousin and she knew what was up between me and D."

"So this is D's fault?"

"No, it's no one's fault. Look I apologize for what happen. Now if you will excuse me."

"Not so fast. At least tell me your name."

Jazz shook her head at the thought of dudes always flirting. She told him her name. He then told her his name. During Brian and Jazz's convo, she learned that the party was for his twin brother. She also learned that he was a Marine and would be stationed in Cali for a few months. He gave her his card and asked her to call him if time permits. Jazz said that she may and got in Peter's 745 and left. Brian walked back in the house. Neither him or Jazz noticed mask men watching them. After being on the road for twenty minutes, Jazz's tire blew out. "Dammit; not now." She cried. She looked in her purse and got her cell. There was only one bar left and it was red. She called Peter and he called AAA on three way. After her and Peter talked to her until her battery died.

Back in Malibu

After Jazz left, Yay went to the bathroom to call Peter. She couldn't wait to get him on the line so she could let him know how stupid he is. She pulled her Blackberry from her bag and dialed Peter's number. No time for Yay-Yay's drama, Peter sent her to voicemail. She called back two more times and was sent to voicemail again: by that time she figured out Peter was doing it intentionally. That was fine with her, one way or the other she was about to burst his bubble by letting him know that the bitch he thought was so innocent, the tramp he gave her job to; is not who he thinks she is. *So she left him a message telling him what she found out when she saw Jazz at the hospital and what had just went down.. That was not good enough. She decided to call Jazz;* without ringing, Jazz's phone went straight to voicemail. Yay assumed her phone was dead. She would curse her out another day. She put her phone back inside her bag, and looked herself over in the mirror; she needed more make-up. She went in her bag and pulled out another bag that contained her make-up products. After applying her make-up, she retrieved her Summer's Eve wipes, and used them to wipe under her arms and between her legs. That's one thing she did not play: bad hygiene. Enough with the bullshit she thought, it was time to make that money... Yay stepped out the bathroom and down

the hall. She walked into the second room on the right; that's where she kept her stuff. She walked in the room and sat her bag on the bed.

When she turned around, there stood the red head dude that had been watching her the entire night.

"What the hell?" She said with her hand on her chest. "Can I help you?" She asked."

"Did I scare you?" The redhead asked.

She gave him a strange look before she responded by saying,

"A little. Anyway I was just leaving."

She then began to walk pass the guy but he stopped her.

"Hey, not so fast." he told her.

"Look, I got money to make and if you ain't spending no money, then I have no time." She stood there with her hands on her hips. He didn't say anything, instead he looked at her with that same goofy smile, but this time she noticed lust in his eyes. He kind of made her uncomfortable. She wouldn't let him know that.

"After I put on my last show, I'll come check you out. Maybe then you will know what to say or what to do. Now if you will excuse me." Again she tried to walk past him and out the room.

"Not so fast." he said and gripped her by her hair.

"You better let my muthafucking hair go." Yay demanded.

The red head placed his knife to her neck and whispered in her ear,

"Not until I get what I want."

****

It took an hour for AAA to come and change Jazz's flat and another hour for her to get back to Peter's place. After what happened, she really didn't feel like being around Peter. To make matters worse, all he talked about while she was waiting for AAA was how he missed her and wanted to lick on her clit. She was so happy her battery died. She didn't want Peter to taste or touch her. It wasn't nothing he did, besides fuck up, and caused her to run into another man's arms. A man that knows what to say and when to say it. A man that makes her smile, a man that calls her just to say how pretty she is, a man that acts like she is the only woman in the world when they are together. A man that's his self when they're alone and around other people, a man that she gave her love to.... a man that wouldn't take her love for granted like Pete did. But there was one thing D and P had in common, they showed interest in Yay-Yay..... Ughhhhhhhhhh...

I know this boy didn't go to sleep without even making sure I made it home? Jazz thought. When she pulled up to Peter's house, all the lights were off. Jazz got out the car and walked up on the front porch, reached in her purse and retrieved her keys. She then unlocked the front door, walked inside and shut the door.

"Peter." She called out. Instead of hearing a response from Peter, she heard moaning coming from the den. It was a girl's voice. She then heard Peter's voice, "suck this dick, bitch, and suck it." Jazz stood still. She couldn't believe what she was hearing. *I can't believe this muthafucka.*

"You wanna swallow it? You wanna swallow daddy's nut? No, get up and let me fuck this pussy. Jazz shook her head in disbelief. She wondered who Peter was fucking. I bet it's that nasty bitch Sabrina. I saw that bitch looking at me when I left. She didn't want to, but she had to see with her own eyes. She needed to prove that Peter was a scandalous ass nigga. And no, the sounds she was hearing wasn't enough to confirm it. She took a few deep breathes and began to walk toward the den. She then heard a familiar voice. "Ohhhhh daddy, fuck this pussy," the familiar female voice cried. It couldn't be. No that's impossible, Jazz thought; these are some dirty muthafuckas. Jazz walked in that den and froze in shock. Peter wasn't fucking anybody. He was sitting in the chair sleep with his dick in his hand. "This my pussy. I own this shit don't I?" Peter said. "Yesssssssssss...." Yay-Yay screamed. Jazz looked at the T.V. It was Peter and Yay-Yay fucking, and there was another person watching; it was her friend, Paris. "You nasty son of a bitch." Jazz screamed and charged at Peter.

Peter jumped in shock. He looked at Jazz and wondered what was going on.

"I'm about to cummm....Ohhh shit........" He heard Yay's voice and remembered he got horny and needed to bust a nut. He forgot to turn off the porno.

"I hate you. I hope you die. You nasty son of a bitch." Jazz screamed.

Peter tried to grab her, but it was hard for him to because of the two cast on his legs.

"Don't you ever fucking touch me. Don't call me. Don't say shit to me. Act like we never met. That's what I'm going to do. You fucking bastard."

"Jazz, I'm sorry." Peter said.

He was disgusting sitting there with his dick hanging out of his boxers. She frowned up her face and shook her head.

"You are sorry. You're a sorry, nasty, son of a bitch." She then began to walk out the door.

"What about you?" Peter said.

Jazz stopped in her tracks. "Me, what about me? You're kidding right?"

"You gave Diesel what you were supposed to be saving for me." Jazz chuckled. "Did Yay tell you that? Well guess what, I sure in the fuck did." She walked out with her head held high.

As she was leaving, Ken was walking up. Jazz didn't even acknowledge him. She hurried to Peter's 745, unlocked the door, jumped in and went home. The night was too much for her; she needed her mommy. When she got home, she took a hot shower, went to her mother's room to see if she was home, she was, but was sleep. She shut her mother's door back and went to her room and went to sleep.

Back in Malibu

It was now 4am and the party was over. The only ones that were left in the Malibu beach-front was Arizona draft pick, Mike Sanders, his female for the night, his twin brother Brian Sanders, Diesel and Savanna. Which was perfect. Now Savanna was able to put her plan in motion. The original plan, per Wack, was to do this party with Yay-Yay and a few other girls from the club. While those hoes were entertaining, she was supposed to check out the house for cameras, safes and anything of value. Which she did. That she knew of, there were no cameras. Safes, she did find out there was at least one in the house. The rich dummy mentioned it when he informed his party guest that he was going to retrieve money to tip the strippers. She didn't know exactly what room it was in, but it was in one of the rooms. Once Wack and his goons came in, they would find out where it was. She had done her part. She looked at Diesel. He was beginning to loosen up. He had been in a shitty mood ever since Jazz showed up. It was obvious that he had some type of feelings for her and from the tears she saw run down Jazz's face, and the way Jazz slapped the shit out of Yay-Yay, she had feelings for him too. Again, that wasn't her business. What they had was between them three. Now that Yay was gone and Wack had no way of knowing how many people were left in the house, unless he came inside, which he wasn't going to do until she gave the green light, she was about to seduce Diesel. Not because she wanted to be with him, no, that wasn't it. She thought he was cool and really cute, but the only thing he was good for was money, and she wanted some. Not just the money Wack was going to give her for setting him and his friends up, nope, she wanted her own. She was tired of living with Wack, fucking him and others whenever he said so. No, Savanna, wanted no more parts of the lifestyle...she watched Diesel as he began to loosen up. Before she slipped something in his drink, he was so uptight. All he did was sit on the couch, drink beer and stare into space. Now he was smiling and looking around the house asking where everyone was at.

"The party's over man." Said Sanders.

D spoke in a slur,

"Damn, the strippers too?"

"Yep, everyone but her." He said pointing at Savanna. D looked at Savanna. "Why you still here and everyone else gone? You got a special treat for me.

Savanna smiled; the drug had kicked in; his speech and the way he was looking at her biting his bottom lip confirmed it.

"I sure do." She said walking up on him.

"I'm next." Sanders' twin brother announced.

Savanna looked at the twin and winked all the while thinking whatever asshole.

"Come on and let's give them their privacy." MS' girl said.

"Hell no. We sitting right here. You need all the lessons you can get. Besides I might be next."

His girl rolled her eyes at the comment, grabbed her cigarette off the table and sat quiet.

Dammit, White-girl thought. How in the fuck was she going to get D to screw her bareback with the others around? Bingo...the bell in her head sounded. She excused herself and ran to the restroom to doctor up the condom by putting holes in it. On her way back into the living room, she could have sworn she heard sniffles, like someone was crying. She had no time to waste she had to work on her fortune. Once Diesel nutted inside of her she was praying she get pregnant. She had been taking Geritol for weeks hoping when the day came, she would be fertile enough to produce. When she arrived back into the living room, they had the music playing and the lights were dim. Maybe she wouldn't need the defective condom after all. She thought. Savanna started off by doing a show for the four that was watching. Once she was butt naked, she danced in front of D, giving him all her attention and he loved every minute of it. Like always, Savanna started with giving D a blow job. She stopped right when he was about to burst and quickly hopped on the dick; no one had even noticed or maybe they didn't care no protection was used. Sanders was so turned on by the show, he made his girl blow him off while he watched them. Sanders' twin changed his mind about fucking Savanna once he saw her pale whit pussy, his dick went down. I love black pussy, he thought as he went to grab a beer and went to the balcony to watch the water.

"Hey man", Sanders called after his red head friend who was running to his car. *What the fuck wrong with that nigga? He thought when he noticed his shoes and shirt was off.*

"I hope that nigga can drive home." He thought.

Sanders walked back in the house. Savanna was on her way to the bathroom. Sanders shook his head; that nigga nut fast. He then looked at his brother and his girl; they was still at it. He walked over to the other side of the room and chilled by himself.

In the meantime, Wack and his goons sat in the car waiting on White- Girl to give them the green light.

"What the fuck they doing in there?" Wack thought, as he watched the shirtless white boy fumble through his pockets for his keys.

"You see that nigga?" One of the goons said.

"Yeah, something ain't right with that fool?" The other goon said.

"White boy probably was playing that truth or dare shit. You know how them niggas is." Said Wack.

Wack looked at his ringing cell phone, it was White- Girl....

"It's five of us. None is a threat. The door is unlocked." She said, when Wack answered the phone.

"What part of the house they in." Asked Wack.

"Everybody in the living room. I'm about to go back in there now. I was using the restroom to call you."

"Alright, cool. We're on our way." Was how Wack ended the call.

Throughout the night Savanna had been texting letting him know what was going on. She told him that there was a safe and that Sanders retrieved quit a few stacks from it to pay the dancers. She also told him about other little shit that went on. The only thing she didn't know was what happened to Yay-Yay...all she could think was that she got embarrassed about being slapped in front of everyone and left the party. When she told Wack, he tried calling her but didn't get an answer. He low-key felt some kind of way about her shaking with some other nigga, but wrote it off as a ho being a hoe. "Let's do this?" Wack said, and him and his two goons jumped out the car. Pistols in hand, ski mask over their faces, the three goons baled in silence. The next words they spoke was,

"This a stick up... anybody move without my permission will be leaving here in a body bag." Wack threatened

******

"Oh my God; what did he do to me?" Yay whispered after waking up from being temporarily unconscious. She looked down at her body and she was completely naked. Ignoring the pain coming from her head, when she rose to a sitting position in the bed she screamed, "I'm going to kill you muthafucka, you're messing with the wrong bitch." She looked around the room for her attacker. She didn't see anyone. The room was empty. The bedroom door was shut, but the window was wide open. Yay mind was on getting away. She jumped from the bed, "ouch." She said when her feet touched the floor. It felt like pain surfaced from every part of her body, especially her anus and coochie. She closed her eyes and took a deep breath. She looked down at her feet and her knees began to get weak; there was blood all over her legs. It wasn't coming from her vaginal area tho, it was coming from the cuts her attacker had mad on her legs and feet. That was his way of getting off. *I'm going to bleed to death, she thought. He tried to kill me.* Yay thought as fear took over. She no longer wanted to jump out the window; how about he was out there waiting on her, if not him, another sick fucker maybe out there. I have to get out of here she thought as she looked around for something to use as a weapon. She saw a hockey stick sitting by the door. She walked over to the door and grabbed the hockey stick. She then noticed her bag on the floor. She went in her bag and retrieved her cell, nervously pressing the red and then the green button trying to power on the phone. After a few tries she finally got it. Once the phone was on, she pressed send by mistake and he dialed the last person in her phone log; which was Jazz. Just like the last time, Jazz's phone went to voicemail.

"Jazz, this is Yay; I've been hurt. He raped me. I'm bleeding everywhere...." She cried.

The phone made a beep sound and cut off. Her battery was dead. No time to waste, she grabbed the hockey stick and slowly opened the door. Ignoring the pain as best as she could, she made her way down the hall. Getting closer to the living room, she lifted the hockey stick ready to knock anyone's head off that was not out to help her.

****

Wack and his goons walked in looking like they were ready to kill everything that was moving. They scared the shit out of the Sanders twins and the girl. All Diesel could do was shake his head. How the fuck did this happen? Diesel thought. This had to be an inside job. He looked at Savanna, she could have won an Oscar for the performance she was putting on. All the crying and shaking she was doing, Diesel dismissed the thought about her being involved. "Alright, now that I have your undivided attention, let me introduce myself and the reason why we're here." Without saying a word, everyone looked at Wack. He continued, "I'm the muthafucka that will put a bullet in your head if I don't get what the fuck I came for. I'm pretty sure all of you know what I came for. I want the money, lots of it. So hit the safe, let me get what's mine, and we'll be on our way!" He looked at Diesel. "Where the money at?" Without saying a word, Diesel stared at the gun man. Fuck them, he was going to die anyway he supposed, so why make things easy for them, plus what type of dude would he be to even acknowledge that he knows where the safe is at.

"Aye, this nigga wanna be hard. Show him we ain't playing." Wack told his goon on the left.

The goon walked up to Diesel. Savanna prayed silently that they did not hurt him. The Goon raised his gun. Savanna screamed,

"Noooooo don't hurt him."

Wack looked at the bitch like she was crazy. Had she caught feelings for the nigga? He'll check her once this shit was over. Like he told her, she belonged to him. How dare she give a fuck about another nigga. Ignoring Savanna's plea... Pow.... the goon hit Diesel in the head with the gun.

"Arggggg ",Diesel called out holding his head in pain. Sanders' girl screamed,

"Stop it. Don't hurt him."

"I'm going to kill the nigga if I don't get what I came for." Wack warned.

Both of the twins looked at each other; they wasn't about to let they homey go out like that. Sanders raised his hand like a scared kindergarten student

Wack had to chuckle.

"Tell me what I want to hear."

'" Look I got about ten thousand dollars in the safe. The safe is in the back. Take me back there so I can get it."

"Ten thousand." said Wack. "Fuck I'm going to do with ten thousand?"

"Well that's all I got here."

Wack looked at his goons. The one that that knocked D in the head, was still standing over him with his gun drawn on him. He was waiting on Diesel to make the wrong move so he could cap his ass. The goon to Wack's right had his gun drawn on the Sanders boys and the girl.

"Blood. Go take that nigga to the back to get the money." He told the goon that had his pistol pointed at D.

He then looked at the other Sanders boy, " by the time your brother come from the back, you better had thought about where I'm going to get the rest of my money from." Wack looked at his goon; he yelled in anger, "HIT MY CELL ONCE YOU GOT THE SAFE OPEN. IF THIS NIGGA RIGHT HERE HAS NOT FIGURED OUT WHERE HE GOING TO GET THE REST OF MY MONEY FROM, I WANT YOU TO PUT ONE TO THE DOME."

The goon nodded to agree. He snatched up Sanders and proceeded to where the safe was at.

******

She knew that voice anywhere. He's going to save me... Yay, thought. Hockey stick still in her hand she ran from the hallway to her Savior,

"I'm right - " she never got a chance to finish her sentence.

Pow Pow... Yay screamed as the two bullets pierced her body causing her to fly against the wall. Caught off guard and not knowing if it was a set-up, the Goon that was escorting Sanders shot him in the back of the head. Wack couldn't believe it, the plan was fucked up. He knew he shouldn't have put them trigger happy niggas on.

"What the fuck." Diesel yelled looking at his boy laid in blood.

Savanna was no longer acting, she was shook up. Two people was shot and possibly dead because she helped Wack with this. Didn't she learn what he was capable of when he set up his best friend? Sanders' girl passed out. The other Sanders was crying like a baby. He wanted to run to his brother and hold him but there was a gun pointed at his head. As calm as he could, Wack spoke,

"I need you to take me the safe. Try anything and you going to be with your brother."

He grabbed the twin and they walked to the back. When they got by the two bodies, the twin dropped to his knees grabbing on his brother. Crying, telling him not to leave him... Wack didn't even trip off it. He was in shock his damn self. The girl his goon shot was Yay. Why were cuts all over her body, what happened to her, did one of these niggas rape her? Angry at the thought, he snatched Sanders up. He wanted answers, but it was a possibility that he would have gave his self away. That wasn't important at the time; what was important was him getting the money and getting out quick so Yay could get help. Her stomach was still moving so he was sure that she had a chance at surviving.

To be continued................

The author thanks each and every one of you for your support. She asks that you leave a review on Amazon, Barnes & Noble, GoodReads, and/or Smashwords.

Sneak Peak >>>>>>>>>>>>>>>

Salty 2

Savanna called Paris and Paris called Yay-Yay's mother. Yay's mother called Mrs. Lewis, which is Calvin's mother; you know Jazz's grandmother? Diesel called Jazz, but got her voicemail, so he called his sister Laurie. Laurie tried reaching Jazz, but she too got her voicemail. Laurie called Peter, but Peter said he had not talked to her. She then told Peter that her brother said that Yay had been shot and she is not looking to live. Peter Panicked. He was grateful that Ken was there so he could help him get to the hospital. Peter and Laurie hung up the phone. Peter wasn't worrying about being on house arrest,; he had to be at the hospital to make sure Yay was ok and to support Jazz if she let him. Laurie wasn't going for Yay, she was going to be a support for her brother. He lost his friend and suffered from a concussion.

Peter and Ken couldn't believe it. Damn, any one of them could have been there. Jazz could have been there, Ken thought! Damn!

 Fifteen minutes after the call, Peter and Ken made it to Pam's house. When Ken told Pam what happened she began crying. She ran to Jazz's room and woke her up and told her what happened. Jazz wanted to hate her cousin, she wanted to say that was good for her, and that God don't like ugly. But that was her cousin. There wasn't any way that she wouldn't be there. She immediately jumped up and got dressed.

 Ken knew that Pam would not be able to drive; he assumed that Jazz wouldn't be able to either. So, he waited until both Pam and Jazz came down and offered them a ride to the hospital. Pam agreed. Remembering what Pete told him about what had went down between him and Jazz, he looked at her and spoke with a sincere tone,

"Pete in the car." He told Jazz.

Jazz frowned her face thinking about him. How did he know about her being shot? How they know to call Peter? They must have known the two messed around thought Jazz.

"Peter is not a factor in my life. My cousin is my concern." She said.

Pam made a mental note to find out what was going on.

Pam, Jazz, Peter, and Ken made their way into the emergency room. The first person Pam noticed was her sister, at least she was there, but she could have called me and told me what was going on Pam thought. And what the hell is this old hag doing up hear? She was referring to Jazz's grandmother. Just as Pam and the rest of them made their way over to where her sister, Jazz's grandmother, Mrs. Lewis, and Yay's friend Paris was sitting a tall blue eyed man walked up on the family. He introduced himself as the doctor, and then began to update the family on Yay's status. He told them that there was a bullet in her neck that couldn't be removed because it was too close to a vein. That was the least of their worry for now. He needed blood. The bullet that hit her in the stomach, mixed with the blood she lost from her cuts, and how long she bled before help arrived, caused her to lose a tremendous amount of blood.

"This white ass hospital with all these rich folks and y'all ain't got no blood? I bet if she was white y'all would make sure she had plenty blood."

The way everyone looked at Paris she should have known she sounded stupid. If she didn't, she knew to shut the fuck up. The doctor continued,

"She has a rare blood type. We're calling around trying to find blood now. Do you know if any of you are a match?"

Jazz's grandmother said,

"Jazz is a match."

Pam's heart dropped. She looked at Jazz's grandmother with a look that said,

"bitch, you knew."

Jazz's grandmother looked at Pam with a smirk and rolled her eyes.

Jazz looked at the two women confused.

"Are you sure?" The doctor asked.

"Yes, I'm sure. They have the same blood type as their father." She stated matter-of-factly.

To Learn more about White-Girl and Wack check out my other titles:

ZipCodez A Watts and Compton Tale

My Story (Drama In The Codez) Savanna story.

Codez2Codez A Watts and Compton Saga

CPSIA information can be obtained at www.ICGtesting.com
Printed in the USA
LVOW101640040613

336938LV00018B/850/P